How
to Travel
with a
Salmon

and Other Essays

UMBERTO ECO

How to Travel with a Salmon

and Other Essays

*Translated
from the Italian
by William Weaver*

Secker & Warburg
London

First published in Great Britain in 1994
by Martin Secker & Warburg Limited,
an imprint of Reed Consumer Books Limited,
Michelin House, 81 Fulham Road, London SW3 6RB
and Auckland, Melbourne, Singapore and Toronto

A CIP catalogue record for this book
is available from the British Library
ISBN 0 436 20120 8

Printed and bound in Great Britain
by Clays Ltd, St Ives PLC

Contents

Preface

Between 1959 and 1961 I was responsible for a regular column entitled "Diario minimo" in the literary magazine *Il Verri*, edited by Luciano Anceschi. The very existence of the column represented an act of courage on Anceschi's part, because cultural reviews in those days took themselves very seriously indeed, and the "Diario," on the other hand, consisted of droll observations on contemporary life, bookish parodies, fantasies, and various lunacies by a number of contributors, among them many of Italy's most gifted younger poets, critics, philosophers, and novelists. We also ran clippings from newspapers, eccentric quotations, and so on, which, as I recall, various contributors to the magazine turned in occasionally, to enrich the column. Since I was in charge, I contributed more than anyone else: at first, moralities, then, increasingly, literary pastiches.

Around 1962 the editor and poet Vittorio Sereni asked me to collect these pieces of mine in a volume for the publisher Mondadori, and as the column no longer existed and "Diario minimo" had become virtually a generic term, I used this title for the book that came out first in 1963 and was reprinted in 1975. For this later edition, which eliminated many of the moralities (some of them were too closely linked to transitory events), I favored the pastiches, including several more recent pieces. Some years afterwards, the volume was adapted into English and entitled *Misreadings*.

That first *Diario* has had quite a history; it has gone through several editions, and I know that the students of several architecture departments are required to ponder the "Paradox of Porta Ludovica," and a department of classical philology created a seminar to discuss whether scholars of the ancient world look on the Greek lyric poets in the way my Eskimos of the next millennium looked on the contents of a tattered collection of popular song texts. Parisian friends, founders of Transcultura, an organization that imports African and Asian anthropologists to study European cities, say that their program was inspired by my "Industry and Sexual Repression in a Po Valley Society," in which Melanesian anthropologists analyzed the primitive Milanese by sophisticated phenomenological parameters.

But, that little volume aside, I have written other "minimal diaries." They appeared in other guises or remained in a desk drawer after I subjected friends to them, frequently co-authors or, at least, prompters. Indeed, after almost apologizing for the first little volume, as if it was less than serious to pursue the pathways of parody, I have since continued with righteous boldness, convinced that it was not only a legitimate procedure but actually a sacred duty.

Almost thirty years went by, the desk drawers became crammed with abandoned manuscripts, and friends kept asking me what had become of certain pieces that only an oral tradition had kept alive. So now I have published a second *Diario minimo*, still convinced of what I wrote in concluding the preface to the first, in 1975: "For such is the fate of parody: it must never fear exaggerating. If it strikes home, it will only prefigure something that others will then do without a smile—and without a blush—in steadfast, virile seriousness."

I should add only that not all the pieces here are in the vein of parody. I have included also pure divertissements, with no critical or moralistic intentions. But I feel no need for ideological justification.

This introduction does not include any acknowledgments: I refer the reader to the piece entitled "How to Write an Introduction" on page 172.

Milan, 5 January 1992

How
to Travel
with a
Salmon

According to the newspapers, there are two main problems besetting the modern world: the invasion of the computer, and the alarming expansion of the Third World. The newspapers are right, and I know it.

My recent journey was brief: one day in Stockholm and three in London. In Stockholm, taking advantage of a free hour, I bought a smoked salmon, an enormous one, dirt cheap. It was carefully packaged in plastic, but I was told that, if I was traveling, I would be well advised to keep it refrigerated. Ha. Just try.

Happily, in London, my publisher made me a reservation in a deluxe hotel; a room equipped with minibar. But on arriving at the hotel, I had the impression I was entering a foreign legation in Peking during the Boxer rebellion: whole families camping out in the lobby, travelers wrapped in blankets sleeping amid their luggage. I questioned the staff, all of them

Indians except for a few Malayans, and I was told that just the previous day, in this grand hotel, a computerized system had been installed and, before all the kinks could be eliminated, had broken down for two hours. There was no way of telling which rooms were occupied and which were free. I would have to wait.

Towards evening the system was back up, and I managed to get into my room. Worried about my salmon, I removed it from the suitcase and looked for the minibar.

As a rule, in normal hotels, the minibar is a small refrigerator containing two beers, some miniature bottles of hard liquor, a few cans of fruit juice, and two packets of peanuts. In my hotel, the refrigerator was family size and contained fifty bottles of whisky, gin, Drambuie, Courvoisier, eight large Perriers, two Vitelloises, and two Evians, three half-bottles of champagne, various cans of Guinness, pale ale, Dutch beer, and German beer, bottles of white wine both French and Italian, and, besides peanuts, also cocktail crackers, almonds, chocolates, and Alka-Seltzer. There was no room for the salmon. I pulled out two roomy drawers of the dresser and emptied the contents of the bar into them, then refrigerated the salmon, and thought no more about it. The next day, when I came back into the room at four in the afternoon, the salmon was on the desk, and the bar was again crammed almost solid with gourmet products. I opened the drawers, only to discover that everything I had hidden there the day before was still in place. I called the desk and told the clerk to inform the chambermaids that if they found the bar empty it wasn't because I had consumed all its contents, but because of the salmon. He replied that all such requests had to be entered in the central computer, but—a further complication—because most of the staff spoke no English,

2

verbal instructions were not accepted. Everything had to be translated into Basic. Meanwhile, I pulled out another two drawers and filled them with the new contents of the bar, where I then replaced my salmon.

The next day at 4 P.M., the salmon was back on the desk, and it was already emanating a suspect odor. The bar was crammed with bottles large and small, and the four drawers of the dresser suggested the back room of a speakeasy at the height of Prohibition. I called the desk again and was told that they were having more trouble with the computer. I rang the bell for room service and tried to explain my situation to a youth with a pony tail; he could speak nothing but a dialect that, as an anthropologist colleague explained later, had been current in Kefiristan at about the time Alexander the Great was wooing Roxana.

The next morning I went down to sign the bill. It was astronomical. It indicated that in two and a half days I had consumed several hectoliters of Veuve Clicquot, ten liters of various whiskies, including some very rare single malts, eight liters of gin, twenty-five liters of mineral water (both Perrier and Evian, plus some bottles of San Pellegrino), enough fruit juice to protect from scurvy all the children in UNICEF's care, and enough almonds, walnuts, and peanuts to induce vomiting in Dr. Kay Scarpetta. I tried to explain, but the clerk, with a betel-blackened smile, assured me that this was what the computer said. I asked for a lawyer, and they brought me an avocado.

Now my publisher is furious and thinks I'm a chronic freeloader. The salmon is inedible. My children insist I cut down on my drinking.

1986

3

How
to Replace
a Driver's
License

In May of 1981, as I was passing through Amsterdam, I lost my wallet (or it was stolen: there are thieves even in Holland). It contained only a small amount of money, but a number of documents and cards. I didn't become aware of the loss until, at the airport, about to leave the country, I realized my credit card was missing. With half an hour remaining before takeoff I conducted a desperate search for a place to report the loss (or theft). Within five minutes I was received by an airport police sergeant who, in good English, explained that the matter was not within the airport's jurisdiction, as the wallet had been lost in the city; nevertheless, he agreed to type out a report and assured me that, at nine, when the office opened, he would personally telephone American Express. And so, within ten minutes, the Dutch part of my case was dealt with.

Back in Milan, I telephone American Express and ascertain that my card number has been circulated worldwide, and the following day a new card arrives. What a great thing civilization is, I say to myself.

Then I tally the other lost documents, and I make a report at the police station. Another ten minutes. How wonderful, I say to myself: our police are just like the Dutch. Among the lost items is my press card; I am able to obtain a duplicate in three days. Better and better.

Alas, I have also lost my driver's license. But this seems the least of my worries. We live in a capital of the automobile industry, there's a Ford in our future, our country's famous superhighways are the envy of the world. I call the Italian Automobile Club and am told that I have only to give them the number of the lost license. I realize I don't have it written down anywhere, except, of course, on the lost license itself, and I try to find out if they can look up my name in their files and find the number. Apparently this is impossible.

I cannot live without driving: it's a life-or-death matter, and I decide to do what as a rule I don't do: find a shortcut, use connections. As a rule, I say, I don't do this, because I dislike putting friends or acquaintances to any trouble, and I hate it when people use such tactics with me. And besides, I live in Milan, where, if you need a certificate from a city office, you don't have to call the mayor; it's quicker to join the line at the window, where they're fairly efficient. But, the fact is, anything involving our car makes all of us a bit nervous, so I call Rome and speak with a Highly Placed Person at the Automobile Club there, who puts me in touch with a Highly Placed Person at the Automobile Club of Milan, who tells his secretary to do everything that can be done. Everything, in this case, unfortunately amounts to very little, despite the secretary's politeness.

She teaches me a few tricks; she urges me to track down an old receipt from Avis or Hertz, where the number of my license should appear on the carbon copy. In one day she helps me fill out the preliminary forms, then she tells me where I have to go, namely the license office of the prefecture, an immense hall, teeming with a desperate and malodorous crowd, reminiscent of the station of New Delhi in the movies about the revolt of the sepoys; and here the postulants, telling horrible tales ("I've been here since the first invasion of Libya"), are encamped with thermoses and sandwiches, and when you reach the head of the line— as I personally discover—the window is closing.

In any case, I have to admit, it adds up to a few days of standing in line, during which every time you reach the window you learn that you should have filled out a different form or should have bought a different denomination of tax stamp, and you are sent back to the end of the line. But, as everyone knows, this is the way things are. All is in order, I'm finally told: come back in about two weeks. Meanwhile, I take taxis.

Two weeks later, after climbing over some postulants who have by now gone into irreversible coma, I discover at the window that the number I had copied from the Avis receipt, whether through an error at the source or through defective carbon paper or through deterioration of the ancient document, is not correct. Nothing can be done if you give them the wrong number. "Very well," I say, "you obviously can't look for a number that I'm unable to tell you, but you can look under Eco and find the number."

6

No. Maybe it's ill will, or stress, or maybe licenses are listed only by number. In any case, what I ask is beyond their capabilities. Try at the office where you first got the license, they say: the city of Alessandria, many years ago. There they should be able to reveal your number to you.

I don't have time to go to Alessandria, especially now that I can't drive, so I fall back on a second shortcut: I telephone an old school friend, now a Highly Placed Person in local financial circles, and ask him to telephone the city's Bureau of Motor Vehicles. He makes an equally dishonest decision and, instead, privately calls a Highly Placed Person at the Bureau of Motor Vehicles, who tells him that data of that sort cannot be given out, except to the police. I'm sure the reader will realize the risks the State would run if my license number were to be given out right and left: Qaddafi: and the KGB would desire nothing more. So it must remain Top Secret.

Another stroll down memory lane and I come up with another schoolmate, who is now a Highly Placed Person in a division of the government, but I warn him immediately not to get in touch with any important officials of the Motor Vehicles Bureau, because the matter is dangerous and he could end up being summoned before a parliamentary investigating committee. My suggestion, on the contrary, is to find a Lowly Placed Person, perhaps a night watchman, who can be bribed to take a peek at the files under cover of darkness. The Highly Placed Person in government is lucky enough to find a Medium Placed Person at the Bureau of Motor Vehicles, who doesn't even have to be bribed, because he is a regular reader of *L'Espresso* and decides, out of his devotion to culture, to risk this dangerous favor for his favorite columnist (me). I don't know exactly what feats this daring figure performs, but the fact is that, the following day, I have the number of the license. My readers will forgive me if I refuse to reveal it: I have a wife and children to consider.

With this number (which I now copy down everywhere and conceal in secret drawers against the next theft or loss) I pass through other lines at the Milan license office. I wave it triumphantly before the suspicious eyes of the clerk—who, with a smile that has nothing human about it, tells me that I must also display the number of the document with which, in the far-off 1950s, the Alessandrian authorities communicated the number of my license to the authorities of Milan.

More telephone calls to old schoolmates, and the hapless middle-rank figure, who had already run such risks, returns to the scene, commits several dozen additional crimes, purloins some information that—apparently—the police would give their lives for, and conveys to me the number of the document, which I also keep well hidden, because, as everyone is aware, even the walls have ears.

I return to the Milan Bureau of Motor Vehicles, and with a few days of waiting in line, it's done, the fait is accompli: I am promised the magic document within about two weeks. By now it is late June, and finally I get my hands on a preliminary document stating that I have presented an application for the issuing of a license. Obviously there exists no form contemplating loss or theft, and the document is the kind that is issued to learners, before they are given a proper license. I show it to a traffic cop, asking him if it entitles me to drive, and the cop's expression depresses me: the good officer makes it clear that if he caught me behind the wheel with that piece of paper he'd make me rue the day I was born.

In fact, I rue it, and I return to the license office, where, in a few days' time, I learn that the document issued me was, so to speak, only an apéritif: I am to wait for another document, one that will say that, having lost my license, I can drive until I receive the new one, because the authorities have ascertained that I previously possessed the old one. Which is precisely what everybody knows, from the Dutch police to the Italian authorities, and the license office also knows it, only they don't want to come right out and say so until they've given the matter some thought. Mind you, everything the office might wish to know is what it knows already, and no matter how much thought they give it, they'll never manage to know anything further. But that's life. Towards the end of June I make repeated return visits to inquire about the vicissitudes of promised document number two, but its preparation apparently demands a great deal of work. I am ready to believe this. They ask me for so many documents and photographs that I can only conclude that this paper will be something like a passport, complete with watermarked pages and seals and so on.

At the end of June, having already spent mind-boggling amounts on taxis, I look for another shortcut. Look, I write for papers with national circulation; perhaps someone could help me, on the pretext that I have to travel for reasons connected with the public weal. Thanks to two Milan offices (of *La Repubblica* and *L'Espresso*), I manage to establish communication with the press office of the prefecture, where I find a kindly lady who expresses her willingness to look into my case. The kindly lady doesn't think for a moment of reaching for the phone: bravely, she goes in person to the license office and breaches the sanctum from which the profane are excluded, advancing amid labyrinthine rows of dossiers, lying there since time immemorial. What the lady does, I don't know (I hear stifled screams and cascades of papers; clouds of dust blow from beneath the door). Finally, the lady reappears, holding in her hand a yellow form, of tissue-like paper, the sort that parking attendants slip under your windshield wiper, nineteen centimeters by thirteen. No photograph appears on it. It is written by hand, with some ink smears from nibs dipped into inkwells straight out of *Dombey and Son*, the sort filled with lees and mucilage, causing streaks on the porous sheet. There is my name, with the number of the vanished license, and some printed lines declaring that the present document replaces the 'above-described' license, but that it expires on December 29 (date obviously chosen to catch the victim as he is maneuvering along the tortuous curves of some Alpine locality, if possible in a blizzard, far from home, so he can be arrested and tortured by the highway police).

The paper authorizes me to drive in Italy, but I suspect it would confuse a foreign policeman considerably if I were to display it outside the country. Oh, well, at least I'm driving again. To make this story shorter, I'll add that in December my license isn't ready, I encounter some resistance when I try to renew the temporary one, I fall back once more on the press office of the prefecture, I receive the temporary document back with, written in a crabbed hand, what I could have written myself, namely that it is renewed

10

until the following June (another date chosen to catch me out while I'm winding my way along a coast road), and I am also informed that a further extension of the document's validity has been approved, since the issuing of the actual license will take a long time yet. The choked voices of my companions in misfortune, encountered in the course of my waiting in lines, have informed me that there are people who have been without a license for a year, or two, or even three.

The day before yesterday I affixed the required annual tax stamp to the document; the tobacconist advised me not to cancel it, because if my license were to arrive, I'd have to buy a second stamp. But in not canceling it, I believe, I would be guilty of a crime.

At this point, three observations must be made. First, I received the temporary document in two months, but only because, through a series of privileges I enjoy thanks to my social position and my education, I was able to disturb a series of Highly Placed Persons in three cities, six public and private institutions, plus a daily paper and a weekly magazine, both distributed and read nationally. If I were a grocer or a clerk, by now I would have had to buy a bicycle. To drive with a real license you have to be Luciano Pavarotti.

The second observation is this: the document I preserve jealously in my wallet is of no value and is very easily forged, and the country must therefore be full of drivers in circulation whose identity is difficult to establish. Mass illegality, or mass pretended legality.

The third observation requires the readers to concentrate and try to picture an Italian driver's license. Since it no longer arrives in its slipcase (which the driver has to purchase on his own), a license consists of two or three pages of cheap paper and a photograph. These little booklets are not produced at Fabriano, like the volumes of Franco Maria Ricci, they are not hand-bound by skilled craftsmen, they could be printed in any printing shop, of the humblest sort, and from the days of Gutenberg Western civilization has been able to turn out thousands and thousands of such things in a few hours (for that matter, the Chinese had already invented fairly rapid procedures with wood blocks).

Would it be so hard to make thousands of these booklets, paste the innocent driver's photograph into them, and distribute them, even by coin-operated machine? What goes on in the maze of the Bureau of Motor Vehicles and the license office?

All of us know that any ordinary terrorist is able to produce, in a few hours, dozens of fake licenses—and remember, it takes more time to produce a fake license than a genuine one. Now, if we don't want citizens who have lost their licenses to start frequenting murky taverns of ill fame in the hope of making contact with the Red Brigades, there is just one solution: employ all repentant terrorists in the license office. They have the know-how, they have plenty of free time, and work—as is well known—is good for the soul; thus with one fell swoop we empty many prison cells, we make socially useful people out of former criminals for whom enforced idleness might cause relapses into dangerous fantasies of omnipotence, and we do a service both for the motorized citizen and for the national petroleum industry.

But this may all be too simple. If you ask me, in this driver's license business there's the finger of a foreign power.

1982

How
to Eat
in Flight

A simple journey by air a few years ago (round trip to Amsterdam) cost me in the end two Brooks Brothers neckties, two Burberry shirts, two pairs of Bardelli slacks, a tweed jacket bought in Bond Street, and a Krizia waistcoat.

All international flights observe the commendable ritual of serving a meal. But, as everyone knows, the seats are narrow, the tray likewise, and the ride is sometimes bumpy. Furthermore, the napkins offered by airlines are skimpy and, if you stick one inside your collar, it leaves your abdomen vulnerable, whereas if you unfold one in your lap, your chest is exposed. Common sense would suggest that the foods served should be compact, not the kind that makes spots. It is unnecessary to resort to vitamin tablets. There are such compact foods as breaded veal cutlet, grilled meat, cheese, french fries, and roast chicken. Spot-making foods include spaghetti with abundant, American-style tomato sauce, eggplant parmesan, pizza straight from the oven, and piping hot consommé in little bowls without handles.

Now, a typical in-flight menu comprises some long-cooked meat smothered in brown gravy, generous portions of tomato, vegetables finely chopped and marinaded in wine, rice, and peas with sauce. Peas are notoriously elusive—not even the greatest chefs can produce petits pois farcis—especially if, deferring to the insistence of Miss Manners, the consumer is determined to eat the peas with his fork rather than the more practical spoon. Don't tell me that the Chinese are worse off. I can assure you it is easier to grip a pea with chopsticks than to pierce it with a fork. It is also pointless to rebut that the fork is used to collect the peas, not to pierce them, because forks are designed for the sole purpose of dropping the peas they pretend to collect.

Furthermore, peas in flight are duly served only when there is turbulence and the captain turns on the "fasten seatbelts" sign. As a result of this complex ergonomic calculation, the peas have only two alternatives: either they roll down your shirt front or they fall on your fly.

As the ancient fabulists taught us, to prevent a fox from drinking out of a glass, the glass must be tall and slim. Glasses on planes are short, squat, rather basin-like. Obviously, any liquid will spill, obeying the laws of physics, even when there is no turbulence. The bread is not a French baguette, which you have to tear with your teeth even when it's fresh, but rather a special friable roll which, the moment it is grasped, explodes in a cloud of fine powder. Thanks to the

Lavoisier principle this powder vanishes only in appearance: on debarking, you will find that it has all accumulated under your behind, managing to stain even the seat of your trousers. The dessert tends to the meringue genre, and its fragments mix with the bread, or else it dribbles over the fingers immediately, when the napkin is already steeped in tomato sauce and hence unusable.

True, you still have the perfumed towelette: but this cannot be distinguished from the little envelopes of salt, pepper, and sugar, and so, after you have put the sugar in the salad, the towelette has already ended up in the coffee, which is served boiling hot and in a heat-conducting cup filled to the brim, so that it may readily slip from your seared fingers and blend with the gravy that has now congealed around your waist. In business class the hostess pours the coffee directly into your lap, hastily apologizing in Esperanto.

Airline quartermasters are certainly enlisted from the ranks of those hotel experts who adopt the only type of pot that, instead of pouring the coffee into the cup, scatters eighty percent of it on the sheet. But why? The most obvious hypothesis is that they want to give the traveler an impression of luxury, and they assume he has in mind those old Hollywood movies where Nero always drinks from broad-brimmed goblets that spatter wine on his beard and his chlamys, or the pictures where a feudal lord gnaws a haunch of meat that smears grease on his lacy shirt, as he embraces a courtesan.

But why, then, in first class, where the space is ample, do they serve compact foods, like Russian caviar on buttered slices of toast, or smoked salmon or lobster chunks with a drop of oil and lemon? Is is perhaps because in the films of Luchino Visconti, when the Nazi aristocrats say "shoot him," they pop a single, compact grape into their mouth?

1987

How
to Go
Through
Customs

The other night, after an amorous tryst with one of my numerous mistresses, I did away with my partner, bludgeoning her to death with a rare Cellini saltcellar. I was inspired not only by the strict moral code instilled in me since childhood, according to which a woman who indulges in the pleasures of the senses is unworthy of mercy, but also by an esthetic motive: namely, to experience the thrill of the perfect crime.

I waited, listening to a CD of English baroque water music, until the corpse was cold and the blood had congealed; then, with an electric saw, I began dismembering the body, trying at the same time to adhere to certain fundamental anatomical principles, thus paying a tribute to our culture, without which refinement and the social contract would not exist. Finally, I packed the pieces in two suitcases of oryx hide, put on a gray suit, and caught the wagon-lits for Paris.

Once I had handed over my passport and a scrupulous customs declaration to the conductor, listing the few hundred francs I was carrying on my person, I slept like a log, for nothing encourages repose more than the sense of having performed one's duty. Nor did customs venture to disturb a traveler who, merely by puchasing a private berth in first class, asserted ipso facto his membership in the hegemonic class and thus his status as a person above suspicion. The situation was all the more satisfying since, to avoid any withdrawal symptoms, I was carrying with me a trifling amount of morphine, perhaps eight hundred grams of cocaine, and a canvas by Titian.

I will not go into details about how, once in Paris, I rid myself of the wretched remains. I will leave that to your imagination. You *can* simply go to the Beaubourg, set your valises on one of its escalators, and years will pass before anyone notices. Or else you can stow them in a niche specially provided for such purposes in the Gare de Lyon. The password-controlled method of unlocking the storage space is so complex that thousands of pieces of luggage lie there and no one ever dares to attempt to retrieve them. But, even more simply, you can sit at a table at the Deux Magots and leave the suitcases outside the La Hune bookshop. Within minutes they will be stolen, and from then on it's the thief's problem. I cannot deny, however, that the matter left me in a state of tension, which, for that matter, always marks the achievement of an artistically complex and perfect operation.

On my return to Italy I felt on edge and so decided to treat myself to a vacation in Locarno. Suffering, through some inexplicable sense of guilt, from a vague fear of being recognized, I decided to travel second class, wearing jeans and a polo shirt with a crocodile logo.

At the border I was assailed by vigilant customs officials, who examined my luggage and personal belongings down to the most intimate undergarments, then charged me with clandestine importation into Switzerland of a carton of filter-tip MS. And finally they discovered that, behind my sphincter, I had concealed fifty Swiss francs of uncertain provenance, for which I was unable to produce documentation of proper acquisition through a bank.

I was subjected to interrogation beneath a naked 1000-watt bulb. I was whipped with a wet towel. I was temporarily held in solitary confinement, chained to my cot in a straitjacket.

Luckily, it occurred to me to declare that I had been a member of the underground terrorist group, the Fascist Black Brigades since its foundation, that I had placed several bombs on express trains for ideological reasons, and that I considered myself a political prisoner. I was promptly assigned to a single room in the Welfare Center set up in a wing of the Grand Hôtel des Iles Borromées. A dietician advised me to skip a few meals to trim down to ideal weight, while my psychiatrist initiated the process of having my status changed to house arrest, because of certified anorexia. In the meanwhile I wrote some anonymous letters to the courts in the area, insinuating that the judges regularly wrote one another reciprocal threatening anonymous letters, and I denounced the Queen Mother of Great Britain, accusing her of having had active relations with the Communist Combatant Squads.

If all goes smoothly, I should be home in a week.

1989

19

How
to Travel
on American
Trains

You can undertake an air journey with an ulcer, scabies, housemaid's knee, tennis elbow, shingles, AIDS, galloping consumption, and leprosy. But not with a cold. Anyone who has tried it knows that when the aircraft suddenly descends from ten thousand meters you feel shooting pains in the ear, your head seems about to explode, and you hammer your fists against the window, yelling to be let out, even without a parachute. Well aware of all this but armed with a nasal spray of devastating effect, I resolved to leave for New York, clogged nostrils and all. A mistake. Once on the ground again, I felt as if I were lying in the Philippine Trench. I could see people opening their mouths but I couldn't hear any sound at all. The doctor subsequently explained to me, in sign language, that my tympana were inflamed; he stuffed me with antibiotics and sternly enjoined me not to fly for at least three weeks. Since I had to visit three different places on the East Coast, I traveled by train.

American trains are the image of what the world might be like after an atomic war. It isn't that the trains don't leave, it's that often they don't arrive, having broken down en route, causing people to wait during a six-hour delay in enormous stations, icy and empty, without a snack bar, inhabited by suspicious characters, and riddled with underground passages that recall the scenes in the New York subways in *Return to the Planet of the Apes*. The line between New York and Washington, patronized by newspaper reporters and senators, in first class offers at least business-class comfort, with a tray of hot food worthy of a university dining hall. But other lines have filthy coaches, with eviscerated leatherette cushions, and the snack bar offers food that makes you nostalgic (you'll say I'm exaggerating) for the recycled sawdust you are forced to eat on the Milan–Rome express.

We see Technicolor films in which ferocious crimes are committed in luxurious sleeping cars, where beautiful white women are served champagne by handsome black waiters who have just stepped out of *Gone with the Wind*. Lies, all lies. In reality, on American trains the passengers seem to have just stepped out of *The Night of the Living Dead*; and the conductors proceed with disgust along the aisles, stumbling over Coca-Cola cans, abandoned shopping bags, and sheets of newspaper smeared with the tuna fish salad that erupts from sandwiches when hungry travelers open red-hot plastic containers radiated by microwaves extremely harmful to the genetic patrimony.

The train, in America, is not a choice. It is a punishment for, having neglected to read Weber on the Protestant ethic and the spirit of capitalism, making the mistake of remaining poor. But liberals are politically correct no matter what, and the conductors are extremely polite even with the dirtiest dropout (naturally I would say "victim of marginalization"). In Pennsylvania Station there are many "non-travelers" wandering around, casting glazed looks at their neighbors' luggage. But the controversy about police brutality in Los Angeles is still in the air, and New York is a PC city. The Irish cop approaches the presumed bum, smiles, and asks him how he happens to be in the neighborhood. The bum appeals to the Rights of Man, and the cop, remarking angelically that it's a lovely day outside, goes off, dangling (not swinging) his long nightstick.

Among the poor, too, there are those who cannot manage to abandon the ultimate symbol of marginalization: they smoke. If you try to climb into the one smoking car, you suddenly find yourself in the *Dreigroschenoper*. I was the only one wearing a tie. For the rest, catatonic freaks, sleeping tramps snoring with their mouths open, comatose zombies. As the smoker was the last car of the train, on arrival, this collection of outcasts had to walk a hundred yards or so, slouching along the platform like Jerry Lewis.

Having escaped from this railway hell and changed into uncontaminated clothes, I found myself having supper in the private dining room of a faculty club, among well-dressed professors with educated accents. At the end, I asked if there was somewhere I could go and smoke. A moment of silence and embarrassed smiles followed, then someone closed the doors, a lady extracted a pack of cigarettes from her purse, others looked at my own pack. Furtive glances of complicity,

22

stifled laughter, as in a striptease theater. There followed ten minutes of delightful, thrilling transgression. I was Lucifer, arrived from the world of shadows, and I illuminated everyone with the blazing torch of sin.

1991

How
to Take
Intelligent
Vacations

It has become a familiar custom, as summer vacation time approaches, for the political and literary weeklies to recommend at least ten "intelligent" books that will enable their readers to spend their "intelligent" vacations intelligently. But thanks to a persistent and unpleasant habit of considering the reader underprivileged and ill-read, some quite celebrated writers take great pains to suggest reading matter that any person of average culture should have read in high school, if not before. It seems to us, if not offensive, at least condescending to insult the reader by advising him to look into, say, the original German edition of the *Elective Affinities*, the Pléiade Proust, or Petrarch's Latin works. We must bear in mind that, bombarded by so much advice over such a long time, the reader has become more and more demanding; and we must bear in mind those who, unable to afford luxury

24

vacations, are game to venture into experiences as uncomfortable as they are thrilling.

For vacationers who will be spending long hours on the beach I would recommend the *Ars magna lucis et umbrae* of Athanasius Kircher, fascinating for anyone who, lying under the infrared solar rays, wants to reflect on the wonders of light and mirrors. The Roman edition of 1645 can still be acquired through antiquarians for sums undoubtedly inferior to those that our former political leaders exported into Switzerland. I do not advise trying to borrow this book from a library, because it is found only in ancient palaces where the attendants are so elderly that they tend to fall off the ladders leading to the rare-book shelves. Additional drawbacks are the size of the book and the friability of the paper: not to be read on days when the wind is blowing over beach umbrellas.

A young person, on the other hand, one who is journeying around the continent on a Eurailpass, and who must therefore read in those overcrowded passages where you have to stand with one arm out of the window, could take with him at least three of the six Einaudi volumes of Ramusio's travels, to be read holding one volume in hand, another under an arm, the third clutched between the thighs. Reading about journeys while *on* a journey is an intensely stimulating experience.

For young people who are recovering from (or disappointed by) political activity, but are still anxious to keep an eye on the problems of the Third World, I would suggest some little masterpiece of Muslim wisdom. Adelphi has recently published *The Book of Advice* by Kay Ka'us ibn Iskandar, but unfortunately without the original Iranian; the translation does not convey the flavor of the text. I would suggest instead the delightful *(Kitāb) al-Sa'ādah wa-al-is'ād* by Abū al-Ḥasan al-'Amirī, available in Teheran in the critical edition of 1957.

But not every reader is fluent in Middle Eastern languages, of course. For the patristically-oriented motorist, less burdened by constraints on bulk or weight of luggage, the complete collection of Migne's *Patrologia* is always an excellent choice. I would advise *against* the Greek Fathers before the Council of Florence of 1440, which would require packing both the 160 volumes of the Graeco-Latin edition and the 81 of the Latin edition, whereas the Latin Fathers prior to 1216 are squeezed into 218 volumes. I am well aware that not all these are readily available on the market, but the reader can always fall back on photocopies. For those with less specialized interests I would suggest selected works (in the original, naturally) from the cabalistic tradition (essential today for anyone who wants to understand contemporary poetry). A few volumes are enough: a copy of the *Sefer Yezirah*, the *Zohar*, of course, and then Moses Cordovero and Isaac Luria. The cabalistic corpus is particularly suited to holidays, because original editions of the oldest works can still be found in small editions easily stowed in hitchhikers' backpacks. The cabalistic corpus is also perfectly suited to the Clubs Méditerranés, where the animators can organize a Cabala Competition, the prize to be awarded the team constructing the most attractive Golem. Finally, for those whose Hebrew is rusty, there is always the *Corpus Hermeticum* and the gnostic writings (Valentinus is best; Basil is not infrequently prolix and irritating).

All this (and much more) will make for an intelligent

vacation. Or, if you want to make things simple, just take with you the *Grundrisse*, the apocryphal Gospels, and microfiches of the unpublished works of Peirce. Or, if you resist intellectual stimulation, stick with Agatha.

1981

How to Use the Taxi Driver

The minute you take your seat in a taxi the problem of appropriate interaction with the driver arises. The taxi driver is someone who spends all day driving in city traffic (an activity that provokes either heart attack or delirium), in constant conflict with other human drivers. Consequently, he is nervous, and hates every anthropomorphic creature. This attitude leads members of the radical chic to say that all taxi drivers are fascists. Not true. The taxi driver has no interest in ideological problems: he hates trade union demonstrations, not for their political orientation, but rather because they block traffic. He would hate a parade of Daughters of the Duce just as much. All he wants is a strong government that will send all private car owners to the gallows and establish a reasonable, but strict curfew—between 6 A.M. and midnight, say. He is a misogynist, but only as regards women who move

28

about. If they stay home and cook pasta, he can tolerate them.

Italian taxi drivers can be divided into three categories: those who express these opinions throughout the course of the ride; those who are silent and communicate their misanthropy through their driving; and those who work off their tensions in pure narration, describing what happened to them with this or that fare. These *tranches de vie* lack any allegorical significance, and if they were told in a tavern the bartender would feel obliged to send the narrator home, saying it was time to go to bed. But to the taxi driver these tales seem odd and surprising, and you would be wise to comment on them with frequent interjections on the order of "It's a crazy world! There're a lot of flakes out there! You mean they really said that?!" This participation does not budge the driver from his fabulatory autism, but it enhances your own self-esteem.

An Italian visiting New York runs some risks if, after reading on the driver's ID a name like De Cutugnatto, Esippositto, Perquocco, he reveals his own nationality. The driver invariably begins speaking a non-existent language, taking deep offense if you don't understand it. You must then immediately say, in English, that you speak only the dialect of your native region. For that matter, he is convinced that in Italy, nowadays, the national language is English. But, generally speaking, New York taxi drivers have either a Jewish name or a non-Jewish name. Those with Jewish names are Zionist reactionaries, those with non-Jewish names are anti-Semitic reactionaries. In either case, they do not make assertions, only pronunciamentos. It is hard to know how to behave with those who have a vaguely Middle Eastern or Russian name, as you can't figure out whether they are Jewish or not. To avoid accidents you must then say you have changed your mind and, instead of the corner of Seventh and Fourteenth, you want to go to Charlton Street. The driver will then have a tantrum, slam on the breaks, and make you get out, because New York drivers know only the streets with numbers and not those with names.

Paris taxi drivers, on the other hand, do not know any streets at all. If you ask one to take you to Place Saint-Sulpice, he'll let you off at the Odéon, saying that's the closest he can get. But first he will have moaned at length over your overweening demands with some cries of "Ah, ça, monsieur, alors . . . ." If you venture to suggest he consult a guidebook, he either does not reply or suggests that if you wanted bibliographical information you should have consulted an archivist-paleographer at the Sorbonne. Orientals are a category apart: with extreme politeness they tell you not to worry, they'll find the place at once, and three times they make the circuit of the boulevards; then they ask what's the difference if, instead of taking you to the Gare du Nord, they've brought you to the Gare de l'Est—after all, there are plenty of trains at both stations.

In New York, as far as I can tell, you can't summon a taxi by telephone, to some club; in Paris you can, but they don't come. In Stockholm you can call them *only* by phone, because they don't trust any old stranger walking along the street. But to discover what phone number to call, you would have to stop a passing taxi, and, as I just said, the drivers don't trust anybody.

German drivers are courteous and correct. They don't speak, they just press the accelerator. When you get out, white as a sheet, you realize why they come to Italy for relaxation and drive in front of you, doing sixty kilometers per hour in the fast lane.

If you set a Frankfurt driver in his Porsche to compete with a Rio driver in his battered Volkswagen, the Rio driver would arrive first, partly because he doesn't stop at traffic lights. If he did, he would see another battered Volkswagen pull up beside him, full with boys just waiting to reach out and snatch his passenger's wrist watch.

In any part of the world there is one sure way of recognizing a taxi driver: he is that person who never has any change.

1988

*How
Not to
Talk About
Soccer*

I have nothing against football. I don't go to stadiums,
for the same reason that I wouldn't go and spend the
night in the basement of the Main Railroad Station in
Milan (or stroll in Central Park in New York after six
in the afternoon), but if the occasion arises I watch a
good game on TV with interest and pleasure, because
I recognize and appreciate all the merits of this noble
sport. I don't hate soccer. I hate soccer fans.

Please don't misunderstand me. My feelings towards
fans are exactly those that the xenophobes of the
Lombard League feel towards immigrants from the
Third World. "I'm not a racist, so long as they stay
home." By "home" here I mean both the places where
they like to gather during the week (bars, living rooms,
clubs) and the stadiums, where I am not interested in
what happens. And for me it's a plus if the Liverpool
fans arrive, because then I can amuse myself reading

the news reports: if we must have *circenses*, some blood at least should be spilled.

I don't like the soccer fan, because he has a strange defect: he cannot understand why you are not a fan yourself, and he insists on talking to you as if you were. To convey my meaning I will give you an analogy. I play the recorder (worse and worse, according to a public statement by Luciano Berio, but to be followed so closely by a Great Master is a satisfaction). Now let's suppose that I am in a train compartment and, to strike up a conversation, I ask the gentleman sitting opposite me, "Have you heard Frans Brüggen's latest CD?"

"What? Eh?"

"I'm talking about the *Pavane Lachryme*. If you ask me, he takes the opening bars too slowly.'

"I'm afraid I don't understand."

"I'm talking about Van Eyck, of course. (*slowly and distinctly*) The Blockflöte."

"Look, I'm not . . . . Do you play it with a bow?"

"Oh, I understand, you aren't—"

"No."

"That's funny. Did you know that, for a custom-made Coolsma, there's a three-year waiting list? So an ebony Moeck is better. It's the best, at least of those on the market. Galway says the same thing. Tell me something: do you go as far as the fifth variation of *Derdre Doen Daphne D'Over*?"

"Actually, I'm getting off at Parma."

"Oh, I see. You prefer to play in F rather than in C. It's more satisfying in some ways, I know. Mind you, I've discovered a sonata by Loeillet that—"

"Lay who?"

"But I'd like to hear you in the Fantasias of Telemann. Can you manage them? Don't tell me you use the German fingering?"

"Look, when it comes to the Germans, I . . . . Granted, the BMW is a great car, and I respect them, but—"

"I get it. You use the baroque fingering. Right. Though the St. Martin's-in-the-Fields bunch—"

There. You understand my point, I'm sure. And you will sympathize with my hapless traveling companion if he pulls the alarm cord. But the same thing happens with the soccer fan. And the situation is particularly difficult when the fan is also your taxi driver.

"So what about Vialli, eh?"

"I must have missed that."

"But you're going to watch the game tonight, aren't you?"

"No, I have to work on Book Z of the *Metaphysics*, you know? The Stagirite."

"Okay. You watch it and you'll see if I'm right or not. I say Van Basten might be the new Maradona. What do you think? But I'd keep an eye on Aldaiz, all the same."

And so on and on. Like talking to a wall. It isn't that he doesn't care a fig that *I* don't care a fig. It's that he can't conceive that *anyone* could exist and not care a fig. He wouldn't understand it even if I had three eyes and a pair of antennae emerging from the green scales of my nape. He has no notion of the diversity, the variety, the incomparability of the various possible worlds.

I have used the taxi driver as an example, but the situation is the same when the interlocutor belongs to the managerial class. It's like ulcers: they strike rich and poor alike. It is curious, however, that creatures so adamantine in their conviction that all humans are

34

the same are ready to bash in the head of the fan who comes from the neighboring province. This ecumenical chauvinism wrings roars of admiration from me. It's as if the members of the Lombard League were to say: "Suffer the Africans to come unto us. So we can kick their ass."

1990

How
to Use the
Coffeepot
from Hell

There are several ways to prepare good coffee. There is
the caffè alla napoletana, the caffè espresso, café
turque, cafesinho do Brasil, French café-filtre, American coffee. Each coffee, in its own way, is excellent.
American coffee can be a pale solution served at
a temperature of 100 degrees centigrade in plastic
thermos cups, usually obligatory in railroad stations
for purposes of genocide, whereas coffee made with an
American percolator, such as you find in private
houses or in humble luncheonettes, served with eggs
and bacon, is delicious, fragrant, goes down like pure
spring water, and afterwards causes severe palpi-
tations, because one cup contains more caffeine than
four espressos.

Swill-coffee is something apart. It is usually made
from rotten barley, dead men's bones, plus a few genuine coffee beans fished out of the garbage bins of a Celtic

dispensary. It is easily recognized by its unmistakable odor of feet marinated in dishwater. It is served in prisons, reform schools, sleeping cars, and luxury hotels. Of course, if you stay at the Plaza Majestic, at the Maria Jolanda & Brabante, at the Des Alpes et Des Bains, you can actually order an espresso, but when it arrives in your room it is almost covered by a sheet of ice. To avoid this mishap you ask instead for the Continental Breakfast, and you lie back, prepared to savor the pleasure of having the day's first meal in bed.

The Continental Breakfast consists of two rolls, one croissant, orange juice (in homeopathic measure), a curl of butter, a little pot of blueberry preserve, another of honey, and one of apricot jam, a jug of milk, now cold, a bill totaling a hundred thousand lire, and a devilish pot full of swill. The pots used by normal people—or the good old coffee makers from which you pour the fragrant beverage directly into the cup— allow the coffee to descend through a narrow nozzle or beak, whereas the upper part includes some safety device that keeps the lid closed. The Grand Hôtel and wagon-lits swill arrives in a pot with a very wide beak—like a deformed pelican's—and with an extremely mobile lid, so devised that—drawn by an irrepressible *horror vacui*—it slides automatically downwards when the pot is tilted. These two devices allow the hellish pot to pour half the coffee immediately onto the rolls and jam and then, thanks to the sliding lid, to scatter the rest over the sheets. In sleeping cars the pots can be of cheaper manufacture, because the movement of the train itself assists in the scattering of the coffee; in hotels, on the other hand, the pot must be of china to make the sliding of the lid easier, but still devastating.

As to the origin and purpose of the coffeepot from hell, there are two schools of thought. The school of Freiburg asserts that this device allows the hotel to demonstrate, with fresh sheets, that your bed has been duly re-made. The school of Bratislava insists that the motivation is moralistic (cf. Max Weber, *The Protestant Ethic and the Spirit of Catholicism*): the hellish coffeepot prevents any lazing in bed because it is very uncomfortable to eat a brioche, already steeped in coffee, when you are wrapped in coffee-soaked sheets.

The hellish coffeepot is not for sale to individuals, but is produced exclusively for the great hotel chains and for the wagon-lits company. Nor is it used in prisons, where the swill is served in mess tins, because sheets soaked in coffee would be harder to detect in the darkness if knotted together for purposes of escape.

The Freiburg school suggests having the waiter set the breakfast tray on the table and not on the bed. The Bratislava school responds that this indisputably avoids the pouring of coffee on the sheets, but not its spilling over the edge of the tray and soiling the pyjamas (the hotel does not provide a new pair daily); and, in any case, pyjamas or not, coffee taken at the table falls straight on the abdomen and the genitals, producing burns where they would not be advisable. To this objection the Freiburg school replies with a shrug; and, frankly, this answer is unsatisfactory.

1988

How to React to Familiar Faces

A few months ago, as I was strolling in New York, I saw, at a distance, a man I knew very well heading in my direction. The trouble was that I couldn't remember his name or where I had met him. This is one of those sensations you encounter especially when, in a foreign city, you run into someone you met back home, or vice versa. A face out of context creates confusion. Still, that face was so familiar that, I felt, I should certainly stop, greet him, converse; perhaps he would immediately respond, "My dear Umberto, how are you?" or even "Were you able to do that thing you were telling me about?" And I would be at a total loss. It was too late to flee. He was still looking at the opposite side of the street, but now he was beginning to turn his eyes towards me. I might as well make the first move; I would wave and then, from his voice, his first remarks, I would try to guess his identity.

We were now only a few feet from each other, I was just about to break into a broad, radiant smile, when suddenly I recognized him. It was Anthony Quinn. Naturally, I had never met him in my life, nor he me. In a thousandth of a second I was able to check myself, and I walked past him, my eyes staring into space.

Afterwards, reflecting on this incident, I realized how totally normal it was. Once before, in a restaurant, I had glimpsed Charlton Heston and had felt an impulse to say hello. These faces inhabit our memory; watching the screen, we spend so many hours with them that they are as familiar to us as our relatives', even more so. You can be a student of mass communication, debate the effects of reality, or the confusion between the real and the imagined, and expound the way some people fall permanently into this confusion; but still you are not immune to the syndrome. And there is worse.

I have received confidences from people who, appearing fairly frequently on TV, have been subjected to the mass media over a certain period of time. I'm not talking about Johnny Carson or Oprah Winfrey, but public figures, and experts who have participated in panel discussions often enough to become recognizable. All of them complain of the same disagreeable experience. Now, as a rule, when we see someone we don't know personally, we don't stare into his or her face at length, we don't point out the person to the friend at our side, we don't speak of this person in a loud voice when he or she can overhear. Such behavior would be rude, even—if carried too far—aggressive. But the same people who would never point to a customer at a counter and remark to a friend that the man is wearing a smart tie behave quite differently with famous faces.

40

My guinea pigs insist that, at a newsstand, in the tobacconist's, as they are boarding a train or entering a restaurant toilet, they encounter others who, among themselves, say aloud, "Look, there's X." "Are you sure?" "Of course I'm sure. It's X, I tell you." And they continue their conversation amiably, while X hears them, and they don't care if he hears them: it's as if he didn't exist.

Such people are confused by the fact that a protagonist of the mass media's imaginary world should abruptly enter real life, but at the same time they behave in the presence of the real person as if he still belonged to the world of images, as if he were on a screen, or in a weekly picture magazine. As if they were speaking in his absence.

I might as well have grabbed Anthony Quinn by the lapel, dragged him to a phone booth, and called a friend to say, "Talk about coincidence! I've run into Anthony Quinn. And you know something? He seems real!" (After which I would throw Quinn aside and go on about my business.)

The mass media first convinced us that the imaginary was real, and now they are convincing us that the real is imaginary; and the more reality the TV screen shows us, the more cinematic our everyday world becomes. Until, as certain philosophers have insisted, we will think that we are alone in the world, and that everything else is the film that God or some evil spirit is projecting before our eyes.

1989

How to Be a TV Host

Some time ago, I enjoyed a fascinating experience in the Svalbard Islands, when the local Academy of Sciences invited me to spend several years there studying the Bonga nation, a society that flourishes in an area between Terra Incognita and the Isles of the Blest.

The Bongas' activities are more or less the same as our own, but they have an unusual insistence on the explicit, the declarative. They ignore the art of the implicit, the taken-for-granted.

For example, if we now begin to talk, obviously we use words; but we feel no need to say so. A Bonga, on the contrary, in speaking to another Bonga, begins by saying: "Pay attention. I am now speaking and I will use some words." We build houses and then (with the exception of the Japanese) we indicate to possible visitors the street, the number, the name of the occupant. The Bongas write "house" on every house, and "door" beside the door. If you ring a Bonga gentleman's bell, he will open the door, saying, "Now I am opening the door," and then introduce himself. If he invites you to dinner, he will show you to a chair with the words: "This is the table, and these are the chairs!" Then, in a triumphant tone, he announces, "And now, the maid! Here is Rosina. She will ask you what you want and will serve you your favorite dish!" The procedure is the same in restaurants.

It is strange to observe the Bongas when they go to the theater. As the house lights go down, an actor appears and says, "Here is the curtain!" Then the curtain parts and other actors enter, to perform, say, *Hamlet* or *Le Malade imaginaire*. But each actor is introduced to the audience, first with his real first and last names, then with the name of the character he is to play. When an actor has finished speaking, he announces, "Now, a moment of silence!" Some seconds go by, and then the next actor starts speaking. Needless to say, at the end of the first act, one of the players comes to the footlights to inform everyone that "there will now be an intermission."

What particularly impressed me was the fact that their musical shows consist, as ours do, of spoken skits, songs, duets, and dances. But in our country I was accustomed to the idea that two comedians first do their skit, then one begins to sing a song, then both exit as some pretty girls trip on stage and begin a dance, to give the spectator a bit of relief. Finally, the dance ends, and the actors return. In the Bonga theater, however, first the actors announce that a comic skit will now be seen, then they say they will now sing a duet, indicating that it will be humorous, and finally

the last actor on stage announces, "Now the dance!"
The thing that most amazed me was not that, during
the intermission, some advertising slogans appeared
on the curtain—they do this in our theaters—but that,
after announcing the intermission, the actor duly
added, "And now, commercials!"

For a long time I wondered what drove the Bongas
to this obsessive clarification. Perhaps, I said to myself,
they are somewhat slow-witted and if a person doesn't
say "I'm going now" they don't realize that the person
is saying goodbye. And to some extent this must have
been the case. But there was another reason. The
Bongas are performance-worshipers, and therefore
they have to transform everything—even the
implicit—into performance.

During my stay among the Bongas I also had the
opportunity of reconstructing the history of applause.
In ancient times, the Bongas applauded for two reasons: either because they were happy with a good
performance, or because they wanted to honor some
person of great merit. The duration of the applause
indicated who was most appreciated and most loved.
Again, in the past, wily impresarios, to convince audi-
ences of a production's worth, stationed in the house
some ruffians paid to applaud even when there was no
motive. When television shows were first broadcast in
Bonga, the producers lured relatives of the organizers
into the studio and, thanks to a flashing light (invisible
to TV viewers at home), alerted them when they were
to applaud. In no time the viewers discovered the trick,
but, while in our country such applause would have
immediately been discredited, it was not so for the
Bongas. The home audience began to want to join in
the applause too, and hordes of Bonga citizens turned

44

up of their own free will in the country's TV studios, ready to pay for the privilege of clapping. Some of these enthusiasts enrolled in special applause classes. And since at this point everything was in the open, it was the host himself who said, in a loud voice at the appropriate moments, "And now let's hear a good round of applause." But soon the studio audience began applauding without any urging from the host. He had simply to question someone in the crowd, asking him, for example, what he did for a living, and when he replied, "I'm in charge of the gas chamber at the city dog pound," his words were greeted by a resounding ovation. (This used to happen occasionally in the West, as when Bob Hope appeared and, before he could open his mouth to say hello, frenzied applause was already heard in the house. Or a host would say, "Here we are again, folks, like every Thursday," and the public would not only applaud, but split its sides.)

Applause became so indispensable that even during the commercials, when the salesman would say, "Buy PIP slimming tablets," oceanic applause would be heard. The viewers knew very well that there was no one in the studio with the salesman, but the applause was necessary; otherwise the program would have seemed contrived, and the viewers would switch channels. The Bongas want television to show them real life, as it is lived, without pretence. The applause comes from the audience (which is like us), not from the actor (who is pretending), and it is therefore the only guarantee that television is a window open on the world. The Bongas are currently preparing a program created entirely by actors applauding; it will be entitled *TeleTruth*. In order to feel that their feet are firmly on the ground, the Bongas now applaud all the time, even when they are not watching TV. They applaud at funerals, not because they are pleased or because they want to please the dear departed, but so as not to feel like shadows among other shadows, to make sure they are alive and real, like the images they see on the tiny screen. One day I was visiting a Bonga house when a relative entered, saying, "Granny was just run over by a truck!" The others all sprang to their feet and clapped wildly.

I cannot say that the Bongas are our inferiors. Indeed, one of them told me that they plan to conquer the world. And this idea is not entirely Platonic, as I realized when I came home. That evening I turned on the TV and I saw a host introducing the girls who assisted him, then announcing that he would do a comic monologue, and concluding with: "And now our ballet!" A distinguished gentleman, debating grave political problems with another distinguished gentleman, at a certain point broke off to say, "And now, a break for the commercials." Some entertainers even introduced the audience. Others, the camera that was filming them. Everyone applauded.

Distressed, I left the house and went to a restaurant famous for its nouvelle cuisine. The waiter arrived, bringing me three leaves of lettuce. And he said, "This is our macédoine of laitue lombarde, dotted with rughetta from Piedmont, finely chopped and dressed with sea salt, marinaded in the balsamic vinegar of the house, anointed with first-pressing virgin olive oil from Umbria."

1987

46

How Not to Know the Time

The watch whose description I am reading (Patek Philippe calibre 89) is a pocket watch, a double case in eighteen-carat gold, endowed with thirty-three functions. The magazine article introducing the watch does not indicate the price, I suppose because of lack of space (though it would suffice to indicate the number of billions without printing all the zeros). Seized by a profound frustration, I went out and bought myself a new Casio for fifty thousand lire, just as all those who feel a mad desire for a Ferrari go out and calm themselves by purchasing at least a car radio. Anyway, to carry a pocket watch, I would have to buy an appropriate waistcoat as well.

Or, I told myself, I could keep it on the table. I would spend hours and hours knowing the day, the week, the month, the year, the decade, the century, the year's position in the leap-year cycle, hour, minute, and second of daylight saving time, hour, minute, and second in the time zone of my choice, temperature, sidereal time, moon phase, time of dawn and time of sunset, equation of time, position of the sun in the zodiac—not to mention the fun I could have shuddering at the infinity of the complete and mobile depiction of the stellar map, or pressing the stop button at the various dials of the chronograph and the tachymeter, or deciding when I should rest a moment and relax in the assurance of the built-in alarm. I was forgetting: a special indicator would show how much power remained. And still another thing: if I wanted, I could also know the exact time. But why should I?

If I were to possess this miracle, I would have no interest in knowing that it is ten minutes past ten. On the contrary, I would observe the rise and the setting of the sun (and I could do this even in a darkened room), I would learn the temperature, I would cast horoscopes, I would dream in the daytime of the blue dial where I could see the stars at night, but I would spend the night meditating on the time remaining before Easter. With such a watch it is no longer necessary to bother about external time, because that would become our sole concern for all our lives; and the time the watch narrates would be, not the immobile reflection of eternity, but eternity in progress. In other words, time would be only a fabled hallucination produced by that magic mirror.

I raise these issues because, for a while now, there have been magazines available devoted to collectible watches, rather expensive magazines printed on shiny paper with full-color pages, and I wonder whether they are bought only by readers who leaf through them as though they were volumes of fairy tales, or whether the publications are addressed to a public of serious purchasers, as I sometimes suspect. This would mean that the more the mechanical watch, miracle of centuries of experience, becomes useless, the stronger and more widespread is the desire to display, to regard fondly, to cherish as an investment, these wondrous and perfect time machines.

It is obvious that these machines are not designed to communicate the fleeting hour. The abundance of functions and their elegant distribution over numerous and symmetrical dials mean that, to learn that it is twenty past three on Friday, May 24, you have to shift your eyes at some length, following the movement of numerous hands, as, in sequence, you record the information in a notebook. For that matter, the envious Japanese electronics experts, now ashamed of their former practicality, have come out with promises of microscopic dials that will display barometric pressure, altitude, ocean depth, countdown timing, and temperature, not to mention, of course, data bank, telemetric time indicator, eight alarms, money-changing calculator, and hour signal.

All these clocks, like the whole information industry today, run the risk of no longer communicating anything because they tell too much. But they also possess another characteristic of the information industry: they no longer speak of anything except themselves and their internal functioning. The zenith is reached in some ladies' watches with imperceptible hands, just a marble face without hours or minutes, shaped in such a way that, at most, you could say we are somewhere between noon and midnight, and perhaps it's the day before yesterday. Anyway (as the designer hints), what else do the ladies for whom the watch is meant have to do, except look at a device that narrates its own vanity?

1988

Stars
and
Stripes

ASTROGRAM
FROM: GHQ, GALACTIC CORPS, SOL III
TO: ARMY COMMAND ZONE IV, URANUS
PER INFORMATION RECEIVED FLAGRANT EPISODES
HOMOSEXUALITY OBSERVED BOOS FIRST ASSAULT
FORCE STOP ALL RESPONSIBLE MUST BE
IMMEDIATELY ELIMINATED STOP STRICT REPRESSION
URGENTEST STOP
(SIGNED) GENERAL PERCUOCO, CIC, CASINO, MONACO

ASTROGRAM
FROM: ARMY COMMAND ZONE IV, URANUS
TO: GHQ, GALACTIC CORPS, SOL III
CASINO, MONACO
RESPECTFULLY INFORM GHQ THAT BOOS, NATIVES OF
URANUS, ARE HERMAPHRODITE RACE (NO. 30015,

INTERGALACTIC ETHNIC REGISTRY) STOP PRESUMED
INSTANCES HOMOSEXUALITY AS PER DOCUMENTS
SUBMITTED HEREWITH ARE HENCE NORMAL
ESTABLISHED SEXUAL PRACTICE CONTEMPLATED IN
URANUS LEGAL CODE AND INTERGALACTIC
CONSTITUTION STOP
(SIGNED) COLONEL ZBZZ TSG, ACTING COMMANDER
DURING ABSENCE GENERAL AGWRSS ON MATERNITY
LEAVE

ASTROGRAM
FROM: GHQ, GALACTIC CORPS, SOL III
TO: ARMY HQ, ZONE V, PLUTO
THIS GHQ RELIABLY INFORMED OF FLAGRANT
EPISODES PUBLIC MASTURBATION AMONG DIGGERS
AND DRILLERS CORPS PLUTO STOP INSIST ON
IMMEDIATE EXEMPLARY PUNISHMENT OF THOSE
DIRECTLY INVOLVED INCLUDING OFFICERS
RESPONSIBLE FOR INEXCUSABLE LAXITY OF
DISCIPLINE
(SIGNED) GENERAL PERCUOCO, CIC, CASINO

ASTROGRAM
FROM: HQ, ZONE V, PLUTO
TO: GHQ, GALACTIC CORPS, SOL III
CASINO, MONACO
CLARIFICATION NECESSARY STOP PLUTO DRILLERS
MEMBERS VERMIFORM RACE (HENCE BORING SKILLS
AND EXCEPTIONAL PRODUCTIVITY GEOLOGICAL
PROSPECTING PLUTO ZONE) REPRODUCE VIA
PARTHENOGENESIS STOP IN CHARACTERISTIC
DRILLER POSITION ANTERIOR EXTREMITY SUCKS

POSTERIOR EXTREMITY PRODUCING SYMPTOMATIC
ORGASM AND SUBSEQUENT SCISSION STOP NORMAL
PROCEDURE CONTEMPLATED IN LOCAL ARMY
REGULATIONS OTHERWISE FURTHER RECRUITMENT
IMPOSSIBLE
(SIGNED) GENERAL BOOSAMMETH AND GENERAL
BOOSAMETH (REQUEST CONFIRMATION COMMANDER
IDENTITY AFTER RECENT TOP LEVEL SCISSION)

ASTROGRAM
FROM: GHQ, GALACTIC CORPS, SOL III
TO: ARMY HQ, ZONE IV, URANUS
AND ARMY HQ, ZONE V, PLUTO
SPECIOUS EXCUSES UNACCEPTABLE STOP EXCESSIVE
LAXITY UNDERMINING GALACTIC FORCES STRICT
TRADITIONAL MORALITY, QUICK THINKING AND
SCRUPULOUS HYGIENE ALSO PROUD TRADITION
MARINE CORPS ROYAL CARABINEERS GRENADIER
GUARDS SUBMITTING MASS RESIGNATIONS STOP ALL
OFFENDERS CONFINED TO QUARTERS
(SIGNED) GENERAL PERCUOCO, CIC, CASINO

Intergalactic Commission for Defense of Ethnic Minorities
Fomalhaut (Piscis Australis)

Your Excellency, I am taking the liberty of drawing to
your attention the episodes referred to in the enclosed
file, which clearly suggests that General Percuoco (a
Terrestrial, I presume) brings to the galactic military
administration a mind-set I would say has been
obsolete at least since the administration of President

53

Flanagan, who (before his unfortunate assassination by an African fanatic) so intelligently defended the rights of marginal races to total equality. As you well know, the Flanagan doctrine decress that all galactic beings are equal before the Great Matrix, irrespective of shape, number of scales or limbs, or even the physical state (solid, liquid, or gaseous) in which they happen to exist. The Intergalactic Federal Government has rightly established a High Commission for Cultural and Biological Relativity, which produces the Intergalactic Ethnic Registry and proposes to the High Court of Justice suitable additions and emendations to the intergalactic laws as terrestrial civilization expands to the farthest extremes of the Cosmos. After the fall of the Great Atomic Empires (the former Russia and America), when the people of the Mediterranean basin, thanks to the discovery of the energy-generating capacity of citric acid, became masters, first of Earth, and then of the entire universe, crisscrossing it with their astrocraft propelled by what a poet had extolled as "the golden trumpets of solarity," it seemed to all a good omen that dominion over the universe had been given to peoples who had previously suffered severe racial discrimination on their own planet. You surely recall the enthusiasm that greeted the Hefner Law, which allowed copulation between terrestrial women and the pentaphallic men of Jupiter—even though we all know the cost in bloodshed of this ill-starred pioneering experiment, which required the no doubt overvigorous males of Jupiter to satisfy five simultaneous urges in conjunction with a single univaginal female. But that undeniable breakthrough nevertheless inspired the intergalactic interracial laws that continue today to be the boast of our Federation.

It is a source of great general satisfaction, too, that our intergalactic military regulations have conformed to the principle of integration and, in fact, have established the principle that citizens should fulfill their military service requirement on a planet other than the one of their birth. We have noticed with great dismay, therefore, that this regulation has for a long time been flouted, as is evidenced by the fact that, like the drillers of Pluto, who serve today only on their native planet, the Boos Attack Force services only on Uranus. This situation explains why General Percuoco, whose military and management skills are naturally beyond debate, is unaware of the anatomical details and reproductive methods of these troops. But Your Excellency can assess the enormity of this diplomatic incident from the television coverage of the consequent uprisings on the two planets involved.

I therefore beg Your Excellency to take measures to ensure the implementation of the intergalactic principle of integration, and I am confident that from the splendid heights of the Moyenne Corniche, and from the Presidential residence, the Palais La Turbie, which affords Your Excellency such an enchanting view of the Mediterranean, a prompt and paternal admonition will be sent to the military command that from the historic palace of the former Casino of Monte Carlo presides over the Galactic Maneuvers, the all-important Conflictual Potlatch.

I beg you to consider me your most devoted subject, and in the name of the Great Combinatory Matrix of the Universe I bend my thirty knees,

Avram Boond-ss'bb

To the Illustrious Polypod Avram Boond-ss'bb Fomalhaut (Piscis Australis)

In the name of the Southern Cross, peace, my dear Polypod. Allow me to answer your letter, on behalf of our beloved Intergalactic President, whose humble PR representative I am, hastening to guarantee the satisfaction of your request, the will of the Great Matrix be done.

His Excellency is well aware of his grave responsibilities as Guarantor of Integration, but he must also bear in mind his equally grave responsibilities as Supreme Commander of the Great Conflictual Potlatch Games.

Through all the centuries of recorded history it has always been difficult to control armies, and the ancient Hebrews actually assigned that task to their Deus Sabaoth. Today more than ever before, this task is overwhelming, if not impossible, in the context of Intergalactic Peace. You know that the greatest statesmen in history, as far back as the twenty-second century of the Christian era, emphasized the dangers of an unruly army of several hundred thousand troops during a transitory period of peace. The great coups d'état of the twentieth century derived, in fact, from an excess of peace (as the late President Flanagan said, only wars are the cradles of democracy and of libertarian revolutions). So you can imagine (but, indeed, you already know) how stressful it is to govern an army of billions of beings from numerous intergalactic ethnicities, in a state of Perpetual Peace and in the constitutional absence both of boundaries to be defended and of threatening enemies to be warded off. In this situation, as you are well aware,

an army not only costs much more but tends to
multiply its component units in deference to the well-
known law of Parkinson. The ensuing difficulties are
easily imagined.

Take, in fact, the cases of the drillers of Pluto and the
Boos of Uranus. The original plan was to include them
in the Lunar Mixed Corps, which, by long-standing
rule, is made up of tractor patrols comprising two
terrestrials (an Italian Bersagliere and a Canadian
Mountie) and two extraterrestrials. You are surely
familiar with the endless problems this lunar
patrolling has caused. The incompatibility between the
two terrestrial bodies was evident, first of all:
coexistence was impossible for two soldiers both
wearing broad-brimmed hats in the cramped
oxygenated space in the forward cabin of the tractor.
And you will recall that the feathers of the
Bersagliere's headgear proved to contain allergens
extremely irritating to horses (this, by the way, may
explain why traditional military wisdom has always
opposed the formation of units of mounted
sharpshooters). But you also know the Mounties'
proverbial attachment to their mounts, which they will
not give up even in a tractor (the attempt to mount the
Redcoats on bicycles ended in miserable failure, as the
traditions of the various corps cannot and must not be
ignored). But that was nothing compared to the
disastrous installation of Plutonians and Uranians in
the rear section of the tractors—not only because the
Uranian Assault Boos' notoriously long tails cannot be
accommodated in the tractor and must therefore drag
behind it on the ground, suffering countless slow-
healing abrasions, but also because, while the Boos
normally live in an inflammable gaseous atmosphere,

57

the Pluto drillers survive only at a temperature of 2000 degrees Fahrenheit, and no compartmentation, however airtight, can guarantee sufficient reciprocal isolation. But the most serious consideration is that the Pluto drillers have a compulsive tendency to root inthe ground and bore (in the petroliferous sense of the word); and while on their native Pluto this activity has no serious consequences, thanks to the regenerative capacity of the terrain, on the moon it promptly led to that condition to which mining experts have given the colorful term "green-cheesing" (endangering the gravitational stability of that celestial body). In short, it was necessary to abandon the integration program and today lunar tractor patrols are manned exclusively by pygmies from Bandar (Bengal jungle), exquisitely suited to this assignment. Functional considerations had to prevail over integrational ones. Bear in mind that this solution is not strictly in line with regulations and is apparently justified only by a temporary order. You will thus understand the extent of the problems the central authorities must face, and I will not conceal the fact that the above-mentioned solution was adopted against the wishes of the Casino High Command. But it is also true that not all military commanders are capable of coping with the countless problems that arise in the administration of an intergalactic army.

In any case, as far as the matter in question goes, His Excellency has instructed me to inform you that he is providing for an ordinary rotation in the high commands: as of tomorrow General Percuoco will be OIC, Quartermaster HQ, on Betelgeuse, and command of the Galactic Corps will be assumed by General Corbetta, the efficient former CO of the

Lancers of Novara. As for the whole Intergalactic
High Command, it will be under General Giansaverio
Rebaudengo, former head of the Secret Services, an
officer in the finest Piedmontese tradition, certainly
ideally suited to assume this complex and grave
responsibility.

We are confident that these solutions offer adequate
guarantees to the Intergalactic Commission for the
Defense of Ethnic Minorities, and special care has
been taken not to choose for this delicate post an
officer coming from a traditionally racist area such as
Africa, Sicily, and the upper Brescia region. His
Excellency is further of the opinion that it will never
be too soon to abandon the legitimate tradition by
which the highest command positions are always
occupied by soldiers of Mediterranean origins, but you
know as well as I do what enormous prestige the so-
called "lemon belt" enjoys. We cannot forget we are
the children of a citric acid technology.

Your most devoted

> Giovanni Pautasso
> Chief, Public Relations Section
> His Excellency the President
> of the Intergalactic Federation

From La Turbie Palace,
Mediterranean

Confidential Report
For: President of the Federation
From: Joint Secret Services, Rome

With some hesitation, I have executed Your
Excellency's order to clarify the position of Agent

Wwwsp Gggrs. I hesitated because the prime
condition of the existence of an office door
coordinating Secret Service activities, always in
reciprocal competition, is the absolute secrecy of its
information. This is a principle we observe so
scrupulously that, as a rule, this office—to avoid
leaks—tries not to be informed of anything being
done by the services it must coordinate. If we
occasionally allow ourselves to learn of some event, it
is only to keep our twenty-six thousand staff members
on their toes, in accordance with the theory of
Institutionalized Wheelspinning, which regulates the
entire existence of the Intergalactic Armed Forces.

In any case, to understand the position of agent
Wwwsp Gggrs, a miniaturized bivalve from
Cassiopeia, we must bear in mind also the situation of
the thirty-seven Secret Services of the Federated
Galaxies. If I may remind Your Excellency, I would
begin with the principle that, if these services are to
function well and if our coordinating office is to fulfill
its task of Disinformation, the government must
remain completely ignorant of everything regarding
these services.

As Your Excellency knows, the Federated Galaxies
labor under the burden of belonging to the
government of a nation without boundaries and
therefore without any possible enemies, and hence
condemned, if you will, to perpetual peace. This
situation has unquestionably created difficulties for
the formation of an Army, though the Galaxies have
been unwilling to give up the idea of having one; they
could hardly be expected to renounce one of the chief
prerogatives of a sovereign state. Hence their recourse
to the enlightened idea of Institutionalized

Wheelspinning, which allows an Army of immeasurable dimensions to concern itself only with its own maintenance—getting around the genuine need for renewal by regularly conducting a Conflictual Potlatch: War Games, in other words.

This solution was not difficult to implement, inasmuch as (even before the Pax Mediterranea and the unification of the Galaxies) the armies of the Vulgar Era had for some time already been devoted largely to self-maintenance. Nevertheless, they had two important release valves. One was the instigation of endless local wars, under the pressure of the centers of economic power, to keep a profitable war economy functioning; the other was reciprocal espionage among nations, whose consequent ongoing tensions provoked coups d'état, cold wars, and the rest.

As Your Excellency is well aware, the discovery of the energy-generating possibilities of citric acid not only caused galactic leadership to pass into the hands of the underdeveloped, lemon-producing countries, but also brought radical economic change, ending the age of industrial technology and mass consumption. Now, while in theory the possibility of provoking local wars remains, their utility has vanished. And this has obviously exacerbated the two major problems of the Army's internal functioning, as it eliminates the normal renewal of the troops (once necessitated by casualties) and the promotion of officers for feats in combat. These serious deficiencies have been remedied thanks to the Conflictual Potlatch, and today our space stadiums are thrilled every Sunday by the bloody clashes between units of our glorious Army, who regularly perform, in amicable combat, splendid acts of bravery and daring, inspired by friendship, the spirit of cooperation, and contempt for danger. Never in previous history had anyone seen young people of every race and social background die with a smile on their lips, without a word of hatred for the "enemy," who in fact is sportingly hailed as a friend and a brother, fighting on the opposite side merely through random selection. And, at this point, I trust I may remind you of the heroic behavior of the Fourth Chameleon Hypertransported Division last Sunday in the Southern Cross Derby. Driven towards the boundary of the celestial hemisphere by the Lions of Serpentarius, rather than clash into the government's grandstand erected on Fomalhaut, it crashed on Alpha, enhancing the Conflictual Potlatch with the annihilation of fifty thousand civilian inhabitants—boldly reintroducing into our War Games the sacrifice of non-belligerent victims, a practice that had fallen into complete desuetude since the archaic Napalm period.

But to return to our problem: while the Conflictual Potlatch has solved the problem of the rotation of troops as well as that of bravery-in-action promotions, it has certainly not solved the espionage problem. Obviously it is pointless for a fighting unit to engage in espionage against the unit it is to face in the Potlatch Galactic Series, because the selection of the forces involved is a matter of public record, readily ascertained via the various military sports publications. But, on the other hand, the non-existence of foreign enemies would risk stripping the Secret Services of any raison d'être: for, just as a nation cannot survive without Armed Forces, so Armed Forces cannot survive without Secret Services.

If for no other reason than, as the Honki-Henki doctrine illustrates, the Secret Services play an essential biological role, allowing an army in order to "burn off" that surplus of generals and admirals who can never be promoted to the highest responsible positions. Therefore Secret Services must exist, and must carry out an intense activity; but this activity must be totally ineffectual and harmful to the self-maintenance of the State. A knotty problem not easily solved.

Now, one virtue of the Honki-Henki doctrine is that it has revived a valuable practice that originated in the area formerly known as Italia, today's Vinotria, towards the end of the twentieth century of the Vulgar Era: the system of reciprocal espionage among the Special Branches.

For the Special Branches to spy on one another there are two ineluctable requisites. First, each must engage in intense and secret activity that the other Special Branches are anxious to know about, and spies must have easy access to this information. The second requisite is the existence of the Loner Spy: a single agent expert in double-dealing and thus able to spy on several Special Branches at once. He can always be relied on for fresh news from an unimpeachable but unidentified source.

But what is to be done when the Special Branches, in accordance with the principle of Institutionalized Wheelspinning, have nothing to do, publicly or secretly? Then the spy concerned must possess a third requisite, namely the ability to collect and redistribute invented information. In this sense the spy becomes not only a conveyor but the very source of his information. In a certain sense it can be said that it is not so much the Special Branch that creates the Spy as it is the Spy who creates the Special Branch.

It was in this perspective that agent Wwwsp Gggrs was suggested as the most appropriate candidate—and for various reasons. First of all, as a Cassiopeian bivalve, he reasons according to a polyvalent logical system and only in sentences of a high referential opacity; the wondrous blend of these two characteristics makes these bivalves peculiarly adept at lying, systematic self-contradiction, rapid manipulation of apparent synonyms, and judicious mixing of terms *de re* and terms *de dicto* (on the order of "if Tullius is Cicero and Tullius is a seven-letter word, then Cicero is a seven-letter word"; a kind of reasoning that, thanks probably to the high level of logical formalization achieved by our officers, proves especially popular even in the most remote garrisons of the galactic outskirts).

In the second place, Wwwsp Gggrs is, as I mentioned, a maniaturized bivalve (like the majority of Cassiopeia's inhabitants, for that matter). It is thus easy for him to penetrate the most unlikely places, compensating for his motor handicap by adopting an appropriate disguise, as a cigarette case or a lady's compact, and slipping into the pocket or the handbag of his contact. Coming and going, passing in this fashion from one body to another while eluding all surveillance, he brilliantly carries out the mission assigned to the Infiltrators of every Special Branch.

Now that the reasons why agent Gggrs was recruited by at least three army corps have been explained, we must still find an explanation of the incident that motivated the request for clarification from Your Excellency's office.

The agent in question, in the pay not only of the Capricorn High Command but of the Antares Police Corps and the Ursa Major Military GHQ as well, while concurrently drawing pay from Capricorn for spying on Antares and Ursus, from Antares for spying on Ursus and Capricorn, and from Ursus for spying on Antares and Capricorn (this would have earned him six separate salaries), apparently inspired by his innate love of intrigue, secretly demanded payment from Antares for spying on Antares, from Ursus for spying on Ursus, and from Capricorn for spying on Capricorn. The impropriety of this activity, which involved each Special Branch in heavy expenditure to buy information about itself, is immediately evident. The deceit might never have been discovered, since the information supplied by the agent was false; each Special Branch head continued to receive information new to him, and thus assumed that this information involved another branch.

But all became clear when General Proazamm of the Capricorn High Command, desiring top-secret information about his own vice-commander, decided to engage Wwwsp Gggrs for this purpose, and called in Captain Coppola, who was paying monthly visits to Pluto to hand-carry the agent's pay to him (the agent, by the way, was being sought by other Capricorn authorities for minor crimes). It was only in speaking with Captain Coppola that the General became aware of the ambiguous situation and began to suspect that there were some irregularities in the organization of the Capricorn Secret Service; he therefore contacted this office, which—simply doing its duty—professed total ignorance of the whole matter. This assertion was enough for General Proazamm, who sensed his suspicions were well founded. Since Capricornians are notoriously telepathic, General Proazamm's suspicions were inevitably picked up by the telepathy agency of the *Procyon Gazette*, notoriously hungry for any bit of gossip. The inevitable public scandal ensued.

We are, however, in a position to assure Your Excellency that the guilty agent was promptly rendered ineffective, and we can assure you he will not be in a position to engage in further missions. In fact, he has been named Executive Secretary of the Intergalactic Commission for the Moralization of Espionage Services. As for General Proazamm, who was transferred to a new post of authority with the Quicksands Bureau of Betelgeuse, we received just this morning word of his accidental death there while inspecting Swamp No. 26. And the *Procyon Gazette* has been taken over by the Citric Acid High Command, which has issued a statement guaranteeing the paper's continuance as a voice of freedom and democracy.

I remain, Excellency, Your Excellency's most devoted

Space Admiral, Squadron IV
(name omitted for security reasons)
Director-in-Chief, Special Branches Coordination

PS. Please take note of the fact that, in conformity with the regulations of this office, all information contained in the above letter is false, for reasons of military security.

Intergalactic High Command
Casino, Monaco

From: General Giansaverio Rebaudengo
To: All Galactic Corps

Officers, semi-officers, soldiers, I assume today the high and complete command of our glorious Army. May the memory of our heroic battles at Gallipoli and the Somme, on the Piave and Monte Cassino, serve as inspiration for our future victories.

Long live the Universe!

PS. To celebrate Galactic Day next Sunday, June 2, in the Gemini Area, a Conflictual Potlatch will be held. The Sirius III Hymenoptera Contingent will be pitted against the Vega Thunder Battalion.

(signed) Giansaverio Rebaudengo

URGENT ASTROGRAM
FROM: COMILITER SIRIUS
TO: HIGH COMMAND, CASINO
RESPECTFULLY REMIND HIGH COMMAND THAT SIRIUS
HYMENOPTERA MEASURE SIX REPEAT SIX
MILLIMETERS HEIGHT AND TWO REPEAT TWO
MILLIMETERS CIRCUMFERENCE, WHEREAS VEGA
SOLDIERS IN THUNDER BATTALION BELONG TO
GARAMANTI PACHYDERM SPECIES WEIGHING EIGHT
REPEAT EIGHT TONS EACH STOP THEREFORE
COMPETITION PROBABLY IMPRACTICAL BECAUSE OF
SCANT DENSITY OF SIRIUS III POPULATION
HYMENOPTERA UNIT MEMBERS FIVE HUNDRED
REPEAT FIVE HUNDRED MEMBERS WHEREAS VEGA
THUNDER BATTALION CONSISTS OF TWENTY FIVE

ASTROGRAM
FROM: HIGH COMMAND
TO: COMILITER SIRIUS
WORD IMPOSSIBLE UNKNOWN TO INTERGALACTIC
SOLDIERS VOCABULARY STOP CARRY ON STOP
(SIGNED) GENERAL GIANSAVERIO REBAUDENGO

Memo to General Giansaverio Rebaudengo
EYES ONLY/TOP SECRET

We take the liberty of pointing out to Your Excellency
that, in the course of our normal rotation of
Intergalactic Units for the honor guard pool of the
Federation President, duty for the current month has
been assigned to the Pegasus Cavaliers of Death. This
office is well aware of the splendid military training of
this brave unit, but must point out that the
inhabitants of Pegasus have a median height of
eighteen meters, and their feet measure, on average,
three meters by two. The fact that they are monopod
does not make the situation less problematical, as
these soldiers proceed by leaps and bounds. During
the inaugural ceremony at the Bari Trade Fair last
week one of the President's guards involuntarily
trampled the Archbishop of Apulia. We therefore beg
Your Excellency to advance the rotation of the roster,
excluding from duty soldiers of ethnic groups not
congruous with terrestrial format.

68

The President further advises against participation in the Conflictual Potlatch by the Orion Runners. As the Orion civilization has developed a system of transmigration of souls aka metempsychosis, the Orionides regard death with extreme nonchalance, and any sports competition in which they participate thus proves extremely unsporting. If their presence is absolutely necessary, it is suggested that they be matched with other units having a highly developed sense of life after death: Swiss Guards from the Vatican, Irish Infantry, Spanish Falange, Japanese Air Force.

> From the secretariat, Federal Palace
> La Turbie

High Command

To: President, Intergalactic Federation
La Turbie

Your Excellency, I do not believe I can implement the suggestions you have sent me through the secretariat. All intergalactic soldiers are equal in the eyes of this Command, and I cannot permit any sort of preference or discrimination. During my long and glorious service as a soldier, I have never made distinctions between rich and poor, Calabrian and Bostonian, tall and short. I remember how, way back in 2482, I firmly resisted the pressure of a bigoted and covertly racist press and assigned Sahara patrol duty to the IV Corps of Inuit Harpooners from Prince Joseph's Land. Those magnificent soldiers died, every last one of them, in the line of duty. When a soldier is in uniform, I give

no thought to his bulk. I am sorry about the
unfortunate mishap of the late, distinguished prelate
from Apulia, but the army cannot make exceptions. In
the long-past twentieth century hundreds of
thousands of Italian soldiers were sent to the steppes
of Russia wearing tennis shoes, but to my knowledge
the prestige of the High Command at the time
remained intact. It is the Commander's decisiveness
that assures the soldiers heroism.

Long live the Universe!

(signed) General Giansaverio Rebaudengo

ASTROGRAM
FROM: HIGH COMMAND
TO: QUARTERMASTER HQ
BETELGEUSE
SHOCKED BY IRREGULAR VARIETY RATIONS AND
ALARMED BY EXCESSIVE CULINARY PERMISSIVENESS
UNDERMINING TRADITIONS AND DISCIPLINE OUR
GLORIOUS ARMY STOP AS OF TODAY ALL VICTUALS
MUST CONFORM TO STANDARD FORMAT FOR ALL
TROOPS FEDERATED GALAXIES NAMELY FIVE
HECTOGRAMS HARDTACK ONE TIN FROZEN MEAT
FOUR CHOCOLATE BARS ONE DECILITER GRAPPA STOP
(SIGNED) GENERAL GIANSAVERIO REBAUDENGO

ASTROGRAM
FROM: QUARTERMASTER HQ
BETELGEUSE
TO: HIGH COMMAND
CASINO
RESPECTFULLY REMIND HIGH COMMAND BIOLOGICAL
DIVERGENCES AMONG VARIOUS UNITS

INTERGALACTIC ARMY STOP FOR EXAMPLE ALTAIR
SOLDIERS CUSTOMARY DAILY CONSUMPTION THREE
HUNDRED SIXTY KILOGRAMS ALTAIR GNU MEAT STOP
AURIGA LIQUID SAPPERS COMPOSED EXCLUSIVELY OF
ETHYL ALCOHOLS HENCE GRAPPA RATION OFFENSIVE
TO THEM SUGGESTING CANNIBALISM STOP HOOKS
MILITIA OF BELLATRIX CONFIRMED VEGETARIANS
WHEREAS CHASSEURS FROM COMA BERENICES
NORMALLY FEED ON LOCAL HAIRLESS BIPED GAME
HENCE SOME DEPLORABLE MISUNDERSTANDINGS
WHEN CHASSEURS DEVOURED ENTIRE BATTALION
MOUNTAIN TROOPS MISTAKING THEM FOR RATIONS
SHIPMENT STOP IN THIS REGARD WE WOULD AGAIN
UNDERLINE IMPOSSIBILITY OF STANDARDIZING
UNIFORMS AS PER HIGH COMMAND ORDER STOP
IMPOSSIBLE FIT STANDARD TUNIC AND LEGGINGS TO
SOLDIERS EIGHT METERS TALL WITH FIVE ARMS
WHEREAS STANDARD ISSUE TROUSERS TOTALLY
UNSUITABLE FOR VERMIFORM TROOPS STOP URGE
PROMPT DECISION RECOMMENDING FLEXIBILITY
RECOGNIZING VARYING BIOLOGICAL DEMANDS
STOP
(SIGNED) GENERAL PERCUOCO

ASTROGRAM
FROM: HIGH COMMAND, CASINO
TO: GENERAL PERCUOCO
QUARTERMASTER HQ
BETELGEUSE
QUIT BELLYACHING STOP
(SIGNED) GENERAL GIANSAVERIO REBAUDENGO

Confidential Report
To: Army Command, Valladolid, Europe
cc.: Galactic Corps Command, Sol III

This Intergalactic Accounting Office has learned that
Valladolid Drivers have been counterfeiting gasoline
coupons and then selling stolen Army fuel on the
intergalactic black market. The disciplinary
committee immediately created by this office, after
eight years' work checking all relevant files and the
invoices and receipts of the Valladolid Accounting
Office, has ascertained that, as of today, nine repeat
nine drums of gasoline have disappeared. The inquiry
has been temporarily suspended because, since it is
conducted by the scrupulous computerists of Boötes,
who on Earth must be kept constantly in
decompression chambers operated on strontium 90,
the investigation has to date cost eighty thousand
intergalactic credits, the equivalent of three million
old Canadian dollars. We request the above
Headquarters to authorize continuation of the inquiry
until those responsible are identified.

Intergalactic Finance Command
Arcturus (Boötes)

Confidential Report
To: Intergalactic Finance Command
Arcturus (Boötes)

At the request of the local Finance Command I have
carried out a rigorous inquiry into the disappearance
of the nine drums of gasoline and have reached the

following conclusions: the fuel was shipped from Bilbao on contraband aerorockets from Saturn and then transferred to Algol (Perseus) where said liquid (high-octane) is considered alcoholic beverage. It has not been possible to identify the whole chain of responsibility because of a conflict of jurisdiction connected with the transfer from Earth to Perseus. On Sol III, in fact, the problem would be handled by the Motor Vehicles Department, whereas on Perseus it is dealt with by Quartermaster. Suggest therefore referring the whole case to the High Command Military Spacetransport Headquarters, Procyon, as per memo No. 376/00/C112, headed "internal contraband."

HQ
Guardia Civil
Valladolid

ASTROGRAM
FROM: HEADQUARTERS
MILITARY SPACETRANSPORT
TO: HQ INTERGALACTIC FINANCE
ARCTURUS (BOOTES)
GASOLINE DRUMS CASE REPORTED ON FORM 367/00/ C112 NOT PERTINENT RESPONSIBILITIES THIS HQ AS AEROROCKETS LEAVING BILBAO FOR PROCYON MUST CARRY OUT RELATIVIZATION IN HYPERSPACE THUS ARRIVING DESTINATION THREE HUNDRED YEARS PRIOR TO DEPARTURE STOP PROBLEM THEREFORE REFERABLE TO MILITARY HISTORICAL ARCHIVE VELLETRI AS PER FORM 450/00/SS/99/P STOP (SIGNED) HQ MILITARY SPACETRANSPORT

ASTROGRAM
FROM: MILITARY HISTORICAL ARCHIVE
VELLETRI
TO: HQ INTERGALACTIC FINANCE
ARCTURUS (BOOTES)
REGRET UNABLE PROCESS YOUR REPORT AS PER FORM
450/00/SS/99/P HISTORICAL ARCHIVE BECAUSE OF
INSUFFICIENT STAFF STILL OCCUPIED CATALOGUING
MATERIAL FOR PERIOD BETWEEN BATTLE LEPANTO
AND BOER WAR STOP
(SIGNED) MILITARY HISTORICAL ARCHIVE

Memo from General Rebaudengo

To: Intergalactic Finance Command
Arcturus (Boötes)

What's all this about some gasoline drums? Gasoline
has not been used as fuel by the army since 1999 of
the so-called Vulgar Era. And what is a Motor
Vehicles Department doing in Valladolid?

Rebaudengo

Intergalactic Finance HQ
Arcturus (Boötes)

General, we quite understand your amazement, but
this Command, faithful to the motto of the
Intergalactic Finance Corps ("hang on"), still has to
process dossiers inherited from former Military
Administrations, all passed on to our Boötes archive.
Actually, the file in question refers to events of
several hundred years ago, but we are nevertheless

able to confirm that in Valladolid a Motor Vehicles HQ does exist. The fact that this HQ no longer controls motor vehicles lies outside our area of responsibility, but we are aware that the National Petroleum Board still extant in Vinotria produces gasoline specifically for that HQ, perhaps in compliance with ancient orders not yet counter-manded. Indeed, we cannot help wondering why a National Petroleum Board still exists, but exist it does, with its main office in Rome, in the same building that houses the Pension Office for Refugees from the African Colonies and the Honors Commission for awards to victims of the Napoleonic invasion.

> Commanding General
> Arthur Arcturus, Arcturus (Boötes)

Confidential Memorandum
From: GHQ, Casino
To: Intergalactic Finance Command
Guardia Civil, Valladolid
Military Historical Archive, Velletri
Headquarters, Military Spacetransport
CO, Galactic Corps, Sol III

Mindful of the motto of my old regiment ("Quieta non movere, mota quietare"), I recommend shelving the entire question discussed in previous correspondence. Respect for tradition is the sustaining strength of our Glorious Army; I would therefore consider it ill-advised and impertinent to question the historical function and the fealty to the Constitution of the glorious Motor Vehicles Bureau of Valladolid, undoubtedly covered with glory in some engagement somewhere in the distant past. If, by venturing to cast doubt on the operation of some heroic unit, I caused the army to sense a lack of trust in its superior officers and in public opinion, the resultant psychological trauma would sap the devotion to duty, the spirit of self-sacrifice, the promptitude, and the morale of both the soldiers and their officers, at every level.

Inquiry shelved.

General Giansaverio Rebaudengo

Ethnic Relativity Studies Center
Alpha, Centauri

To: General Rebaudengo

As the matter of the "Valladolid gasoline" consumed on Algol as a beverage has been brought by chance to Your Excellency's attention, we would point out that this case is not unique. The army must bear in mind the awkward situations deriving from the divergences in prevalent customs and practices among components of the Intergalactic Army. For example, on receiving word of an ophthalmic epidemic among the Briareians of Regulus, the Betelgeuse Quartermaster Corps shipped to that base one hundred thousand hectoliters of boric acid solution for therapeutic purposes, unaware that on that planet boric acid is (illicitly) used as a drug. It would therefore be necessary that the various substances handled by the army be catalogued according to all their possible uses. We suggest use of the Koenig-Stumpf matrix forms, which allow $(83,000)^2$ different combinations.

Dr. Malinowski
Director, Studies Center

Ethnic Relativity Studies Center
Alpha, Centauri

To: General Rebaudengo

Your Excellency, we would like to express our thanks to you for having accepted our recommendations, but we venture to suggest that you may have been over-hasty in entrusting the compilation of the Koenig-Stumpf matrix forms to the Altair mechanographic center. These forms, in fact, posit a non-Euclidean geometry of Riemannian origin and require a modal logic. The natives of Altair, in contrast, think in monovalent terms (for them either a thing is or it is) and measure space according to a geometry known as hypoeuclidean or Abbott's geometry, which posits a single dimension. We would further remind you of the unfortunate incident on Altair after the attempt—despite the Altairians' ability to recognize only one color—to introduce varicolored shoulder patches to distinguish the various units. To be frank, we wonder how a mechanographic center can even exist on Altair, since the natives are unable to perceive three-dimensional objects. In moments of discouragement we also wonder why anything exists on Altair, if it does exist. The only documentation to date of the existence of any form of life on that star comes from the ESP center on Mount Wilson, reportedly in telepathic contact with the inhabitants.

> Respectfully yours,
> Dr. Malinowski
> Director, Studies Center

ASTROGRAM

FROM: GHQ

TO: POLICE COMMAND, CENTAUR CONSTELLATION

AND TO: PLANETARY POLICE HQ, SOL III

ORDER IMMEDIATE ARREST DOCTOR MALINOWSKI FOR
SLANDERING GLORIOUS MILITARY FORCES ALTAIR
STOP ALSO ORDER CLOSURE MOUNT WILSON ESP
CENTER STOP INCONCEIVABLE THAT MILITARY
CENTER STAFF SPEND ALL DAY THINKING STOP NO
LOAFERS GOLDBRICKERS TOLERATED STOP CENTER
WILL REOPEN ONLY WHEN ALL TELEPATHIC
COMMUNICATION CAN BE RECORDED STOP IN
TRIPLICATE STOP

(SIGNED) GENERAL GIANSAVERIO REBAUDENGO

ASTROGRAM

FROM: ADVANCE POST

SMALL MAGELLANIC CLOUD

TO: INTERGALACTIC GHQ

CASINO, MONACO

AND TO: OFFICE, FEDERATION PRESIDENT

LA TURBIE

REPORTS FROM FARTHEST CONFINE KNOWN
UNIVERSE WARN OF ADVANCE UNIDENTIFIED FLYING
OBJECTS STOP FLYING SAPPER PATROL FROM
CANOPUS DESTROYED BY INVADER UNITS STOP
INVADERS PRESUMED ARRIVING FROM HYPERZONE
UNIVERSE STOP THEIR DESTRUCTIVE POWER DERIVED
FROM UNKNOWN ENERGY SOURCE THREATENS
SURVIVAL INTERGALACTIC FEDERATION STOP
INSTRUCTIONS URGENT AS POSSIBLE THE
(MESSAGE INCOMPLETE)

ASTROGRAM

FROM: OFFICE, FEDERATION PRESIDENT

TO: INTERGALACTIC GHQ

FOR FIRST TIME IN ITS HISTORY FEDERATION MUST
CONFRONT EXTERNAL ENEMY STOP PREPARE
IMMEDIATE DEFENSE STOP REASSURED BY NOBLE
MILITARY TRADITION OUR ARMY AND INVALUABLE
EXPERIENCE OUR SUPERIOR OFFICERS IN THIS
TRAGIC AND HISTORIC EVENT STOP GENERAL
REBAUDENGO ASSUMING TOTAL COMMAND
OPERATIONS STOP
(SIGNED) PRESIDENT LA BARBERA

ASTROGRAM

FROM: INTERGALACTIC GHQ

CASINO

TO ALL OPERATIVE UNITS

UNIVERSE

OFFICERS NONCOMMISSIONED OFFICERS SOLDIERS
STOP HOUR OF DESTINY IS KNOCKING AT GATES OF
FEDERATED GALAXIES STOP OUR PROMPT RESPONSE
OUR SELFSACRIFICE OUR EFFICIENCY IN TACTICS AND
STRATEGY WILL DECIDE FATE OF OUR HOMELAND
STOP EACH OF US MUST TAKE UP HIS POST AND
THERE MUST BE A POST FOR EACH STOP ASSUMING
DIRECT COMMAND OF OPERATIONS I ORDER ALL
MOBILE UNITS OF SOLAR SYSTEM TO ENTRENCH
ALONG MARNE STOP IV CORPS ARMY BASED ON
BOOTES, WILL OCCUPY STATIONS OF MAGINOT LINE
DUNKIRK BASTOGNE STOP V ARMY CORPS STATIONED
ON PLEIADES AND SPECIAL UNITS OF OCTOPODS OF
SERPENTARIUS ENCAMP IN ARDENNES STOP ARMORED
UNITS OF LIQUID SHARPSHOOTERS OF AURIGA HOLD

MONTE GRAPPA STOP ESSENTIAL PROVIDE
DECOMPRESSION CHAMBERS AND SOLIDIFICATION
SPACES ABOVE 118 METERS STOP DEATH PERSEIDS OF
ALGOL WILL HOLD LEFT BANK OF RHINE WITH BOAT
BRIDGES READY STOP DRILLERS OF PLUTO PROCEED
IMMEDIATELY TO PEARL HARBOR AND DIG IN STOP
ALL OTHER UNITS AWAIT FURTHER ORDERS IN
WATERLOO PLAIN STOP WE SHALL DEFEND OUR
GALAXY AT WHATEVER COST STOP WE SHALL FIGHT
ON NEBULAS STOP WE SHALL FIGHT ON ASTEROIDS
STOP WE SHALL FIGHT ON EVERY MOON AND EVERY
CONSTELLATION STOP FOR GOD GALAXY AND SAINT
GEORGE STOP

1976

Conversation
in
Babylon

(Between the Tigris and the Euphrates, in the shade of the Hanging Gardens, not many thousands of years ago)

URUK: How do you like these cuneiform characters? My new serf-writer composed the whole beginning of the Hammurabi code in about ten hours.

NIMROD: What did you use? An Apple Nominator from Eden Valley?

URUK: Are you nuts? You can't trade in one of those things even at the Tyre slave market. No, this is an Egyptian serf-writer, a Thoth 3 Megis-DOS. Very low consumption. One bowl of rice a day, and it has a hieroglyphics program, too.

NIMROD: You're just cluttering up its memory.

URUK: But it formats while it's copying. You don't need a separate serf-formatter any more to collect the clay, mold the tablet, and dry it in the sun, while the serf-writer does the rest. Mine molds, dries at the fire, and writes directly.

NIMROD: But this one takes Egyptian 5.25 cubit tablets and must weigh a good sixty kilos. Why don't you use a portable?

URUK: What? One of those liquid-crystal Chaldean screens? That's Magi stuff.

NIMROD: No. I mean a dwarf-writer, an African pygmy as modified in Sidon. You know what those Phoenicians are like, they copy everything from the Egyptians, and then they miniaturize. Look: a laptop. It writes while seated on your knees.

URUK: Disgusting. And hunchbacked as well.

NIMROD: Of course. They inserted a plate under its shoulders for quick back-up. One lash of the whip and he writes directly in Alpha-Beta, you see? Instead of the graphic mode, he uses a text mode. That means you can do everything with twenty-one characters. You can write the whole text of Hammurabi on a few 3.5 tablets.

URUK: But then you have to buy a serf-translator.

NIMROD: Absolutely not. The dwarf has the translator built in. Another lash and he transcribes in cuneiform.

URUK: Can he handle graphics?

NIMROD: Naturally. Who do you think did all the plans for the Tower?

URUK: Can you trust him, though? Maybe the whole thing will fall down later.

NIMROD: What an idea! He's installed Pythagoras in his memory, and Memphis Lotus, too. You give him the surface measurements and crack the whip, and he gives you a ziggurat in three dimensions. When they built the pyramids the Egyptians were still using the Moses ten-commandment system, which required a back-up of ten thousand serf-builders. And they weren't the least bit user-friendly. All that hardware's obsolete, and they had to throw it into the Red Sea. I believe the waters rose up.

URUK: What about calculation?

NIMROD: Oh, it speaks Zodiac. It will produce your horoscope in a matter of seconds. What you see is what you get.

URUK: Does it cost much?

NIMROD: Look, if you buy it here, the harvest of a whole season wouldn't be enough. But if you can get someone to buy you one at the Byblos street fair, it's yours for a sack of seeds. It demands a lot of input, to be sure, but you know the rule: garbage in, garbage out.

URUK: Hm. I'm still pretty happy with my Egyptian. If your dwarf is compatible with my 3 Megis-DOS, couldn't you program him for Zodiac, at least?

NIMROD: In theory that's illegal, because when you buy one, you have to swear it's for your own personal use. . . . But everybody does it. Sure, I'll put them in contact. I just hope yours doesn't have the virus.

URUK: Bursting with health. What scares me, though, is the way they come out with some new language every day. In the end the programs will all get confused.

NIMROD: Don't worry. It could never happen here. Not in Babel.

1991

On the Impossibility of Drawing a Map of the Empire on a Scale of 1 to 1

". . . in that Empire, the Cartographer's art achieved such a degree of perfection that the Map of a single Province occupied an entire City, and the Map of the Empire, an entire Province. In time, these vast Maps were no longer sufficient. The Guild of Cartographers created a Map of the Empire, which perfectly coincided with the Empire itself. But Succeeding Generations, with diminished interest in the Study of Cartography, believed that this immense Map was of no use, and not Impiously, they abandoned it to the Inclemency of the Sun and of numerous Winters. In the Deserts of the West ruined Fragments of the Map survive, inhabited by Animals and Beggars; in all the Country there is no other Relic of the Geographical Disciplines."

(from Viajes de Varones Prudentes, *Suárez Miranda, book IV, chap. XIV, Lérida, 1658. Quoted by Jorge Luis Borges*, Historia universal de la infamia, "Etcétera", Buenos Aires, 1935).

1. *Requirements for a 1:1 Map*

Herein is discussed the theoretical possibility of a map of the empire on a scale of 1 to 1, assuming these postulates:

1. That the map be, in fact, one to one, and therefore coextensive with the territory of the empire.

2. That it be a map and not a plaster cast; in other words, dismissing the possibility of covering the surface of the empire with a malleable material reproducing every relief, even minimal. In this case the project would be considered, not cartography, but rather the packaging or paving of the empire, and it would thus be more appropriate legally to decree the empire a map of itself, with all the consequent semiotic paradoxes.

3. That the empire in question be that X than which *nihil maius cogitari possit*, and hence that the map cannot be produced and spread out in a desert area of a second, separate empire X_2 such that $X_2>X$ (as if a 1:1 map of the Principality of Monaco were to be spread out in the Sahara). In this case the project would lose all theoretical interest.

4. That the map be faithful, depicting not only the natural reliefs of the empire but also its artifacts, as well as the totality of the empire's subjects (this last is an ideal condition, which may be discarded in the production of an impoverished map).

5. That it be a map and not an atlas with partial pages. In theory there is nothing to prevent the realization, over a reasonable amount of time, of a series of partial projections on separate sheets, to be used individually for reference to different portions of the territory. The map may be produced on separate sheets, but

only on condition that they be sutured in such a way as to construct the overall map of the entire territory of the empire.

6. That the map, finally, be a semiotic tool—that it be capable, in other words, of signifying the empire or of allowing references to the empire, especially in those instances when the empire is not otherwise perceptible. This last condition means that the map cannot be a transparent sheet in any way fixed over the territory on which the reliefs of the territory itself are projected point by point; for in that case any extrapolation carried out on the map would be carried out at the same time on the territory beneath it, and the map would lose its function as maximum existential graph.

It is therefore necessary that (i) the map not be transparent; or that (ii) it not lie on the territory; or, finally, that (iii) it is adjustable in such a way that the reference points of the map lie on points of the territory that are not the ones they indicate.

It will be demonstrated that each of these three conditions involves insuperable practical difficulties and theoretical paradoxes.

2. *Methods of Production of the Map*

2.1. *Opaque map spread out over the territory*
As it is opaque, this map would be perceptible while perception of the underlying territory would be obscured, but by creating a membrane between the territory and the sun's rays or any atmospheric precipitation, it would alter the ecological equilibrium of the territory itself. Such a map would therefore depict the territory differently from its actual state. The constant correction of the map, theoretically possible in the case

of a suspended map (cf. 2.2), is in this case impossible: the alterations of the territory could not be perceived through the opacity of the map. Thus the observer would make inferences about an unknown territory from an unfaithful map. If, finally, the map must include the inhabitants as well, it would for this same reason prove once again unfaithful as it would represent an empire inhabited by subjects who, in reality, inhabit the map.

2.2. *Suspended map*
On the territory of the empire stakes would be erected, of a height equal to its highest relief points, and over the upper ends of the stakes would be extended a cartaceous or linen surface on which, from below, the features of the territory would be projected. Such a map could be used as a sign of the territory, since, to inspect it, one must raise one's eyes, turning one's gaze away from the corresponding territory. In practice, however (and this is a consideration that would apply also to the spread out, opaque map, if it were not made impossible by other, more cogent arguments), since each portion of the map could be consulted only by those residing in the corresponding portion of the territory, the map would not allow the reception of information about parts of the territory different from those where the map is being consulted.

The problem could be overcome by surveying the map from above: but (apart from (i) the difficulty of emerging with kites or guided balloons from a territory entirely covered by a cartaceous or linen surface; (ii) the necessity of making the map equally legible from above and from below; and (iii) the fact that the same cognitive result could easily be achieved flying over a territory without a map) any inhabitant who flew over the map, abandoning for this purpose the territory itself, would automatically make the map inaccurate, because it would then represent a territory having a number of inhabitants superior, at least by one, to that obtaining at the moment of the aerial observation. Such a solution would thus be possible only with an impoverished map that did not depict the subjects.

Finally, if the suspended map were opaque, the same objection raised for the extended map would be valid: preventing the penetration of solar rays and atmospheric precipitation, it would alter the ecological equilibrium of the territory and thus become an unfaithful representation of it.

The subjects could obviate this problem in two ways: either (i) by producing every single part of the map, once all the stakes were in place, in a single moment of time at every point in the territory, so that the map would remain faithful at least in the instant when it is completed (and perhaps for many successive hours); or else (ii) by arranging for ongoing correction of the map based on the modifications of the territory. But in this second case, the corrective activity of the subjects would involve them in migrations that the map could not record, and unless it were an impoverished version, it would become unfaithful once more. Furthermore, occupied in constant revision of the map, the subjects could not deal with the ecological decline of the territory; the activity of map revision would lead to the extinction of all the subjects—and therefore of the empire.

A similar situation would arise if the map were of transparent and permeable material. It would be impossible to study in the daytime, because of the glare of the sun's rays, and any colored area that reduced the glare would inevitably diminish the action of the sun on the territory below, provoking at the same time ecological transformations of lesser extent but of equal theoretical impact on the fidelity of the map.

We have overlooked the possibility of a suspended map capable of being folded and unfolded in a different orientation. This solution would no doubt eliminate many of the difficulties discussed above, but, even if technically different from the folding map of the third category, it would prove physically more cumbersome. It would in any case involve the same paradoxes of folding that arise with this third type of map, and would be open to the same objections.

2.3. *Transparent map, permeable, extended, and adjustable*

Let us imagine that such a map, drawn on transparent and permeable material (gauze, for example), is spread out over the surface and is adjustable.

In any case, once the map has been drawn and spread out, either the subjects remain on the territory beneath it, or they climb on top of it. But if the subjects were to prepare the map while it is above their heads, not only would they be unable to move, because every movement would alter the positions of the subjects that the map describes (unless we have recourse, once again, to an impoverished map), but further, in moving, they would cause tangles in the very fine membrane above them, resulting in serious discomfort and once more making the map unfaithful: it would assume a different topological configuration, producing disaster areas not corresponding to the planimetry of the territory. It must therefore be supposed that the subjects have produced and extended the map while remaining on top of it.

In this case we can adduce numerous paradoxes already considered in connection with the previous maps: the map would represent a territory inhabited by subjects who in reality inhabit the map (unless it is a summary, or impoverished, map); the map could not be consulted because each subject could examine only the part corresponding to the territory on which subject and map lie; the map's transparency would eliminate its semiotic function, since it would be functional as sign only in the presence of its own referent; residing on the map, the subjects could not tend the territory, which would deteriorate, making the map unfaithful. . . . It is necessary, then, for the map to be capable of being folded and then reopened with a different orientation, so that every point X of the map representing a point Y of the territory can be consulted when the point X of the map lies on any point Z of the territory, where $Z \neq Y$. Folding and unfolding, finally, permit long periods of time when the map is not being consulted and does not cover the territory, and thus allow the cultivation and maintenance of territory necessary to keep its actual configuration always the equivalent of the one depicted on the map.

2.4. *Folding and unfolding the map*

Certain preliminary conditions must be postulated: (i) that the reliefs of the terrain allow the free movement of those subjects assigned to folding; (ii) that a vast central desert exist, where the folded map can be stored and where it can be turned when it must be unfolded again in a different orientation; (iii) that the territory have the form either of a circle or of a regular polygon, so that the map, however oriented, will not exceed its boundaries (a 1:1 map of Italy, shifted ninety degrees, would be spread out over the Mediterranean); and (iv) that, as an inevitable consequence, the map will have a central point, lying always on the same portion of the territory that it represents.

Once these conditions have been satisfied, the subjects can move en masse towards the farthest boundaries of the empire to avoid the map's being folded up with subjects inside. To avoid potential overcrowding when the subjects are all clustered at the edges of the map (and of the empire), we must postulate an empire inhabited by a number of subjects not superior to the number of measuring units of the total perimeter of the map, the perimetric unit of measurement being equivalent to the space occupied by one subject in a standing position.

Now suppose that each subject grasps a bit of the edge of the map and begins folding it, while retreating further and further. A critical point would be reached at which the subjects would all be crammed together at the center of the territory, standing on top of the center of the map and supporting its folded edges above their heads: a situation aptly termed scrotum catastrophe, as the entire population of the empire is enclosed in a little transparent sac, in a situation of theoretical stalemate and of considerable physical and psychological discomfort. The subjects must therefore, as the folding gradually proceeds, leap instead outside the map and onto the territory itself, where they will continue folding from outside, until the final stages of the folding, when no subject remains inside the sac.

But this solution would inevitably produce the following situation: the territory would consist, once folding is completed, of the original terrain, plus an enormous folded map in its center. Thus the folded map, no longer consultable, would prove unfaithful as well, because it is known for certain that it would represent the territory without its folded self in the center. And there is no apparent reason why a map should be unfolded and consulted when it is known *a priori* to be unfaithful. On the other hand, if the map were to depict the territory with itself folded in the center, it would immediately become unfaithful every time it was unfolded.

It could be assumed that the map is subject to a principle of indetermination, for it is the act of unfolding that makes a map faithful whereas, when folded, it is unfaithful. In this situation the map could be unfolded whenever there was a desire to make it faithful.

There still remains, however (unless we have recourse to the partial, or summary, map), the problem of the position to be assumed by the subjects after the map has been unfolded and laid out with a different orientation. For it to be faithful each subject, once the unfolding is completed, must assume the position he had, at the moment of its creation, on the actual territory. Only at this cost will a subject resident at point Z of the territory—on which, say, a point X_2 of the map lies—be depicted exactly at point X_1 of the map that currently lies, for example, on point Y of the territory. At the same time, every subject could obtain information from the map about a point of the territory different from the one where he resides—and about a subject different from himself.

Toilsome as it may be, and full of practical difficulties, this solution makes the transparent and permeable map, spread out and adjustable, the best prospect, while obviating any need to settle for a summary map. But this map, too, like the previously mentioned ones, falls victim to the Normal Map paradox.

3. *The Paradox of the Normal Map*

When the map is installed over all the territory (whether suspended or not), the territory of the empire has the characteristic of being a territory entirely covered by a map. The map does not take account of this characteristic, which would have to be presented on another map that depicted the territory plus the lower map. But such a process would be infinite (the "third man" argument). In any case, if the process stops, a final map is produced that represents all the maps between itself and the territory, but does not represent itself. We call this map the Normal Map.

A Normal Map is subject to a quasi-Russell–Frege paradox: every territory, plus a map representing it, can be seen as a normal set (the map does not belong to the set of objects that constitute the territory). But we cannot conceive sets of normal sets. Therefore we should think either of a not-normal set, in which the final map is part of the territory it represents (which is false, otherwise it should also represent itself) or of a normal set in which the final map is necessarily unfaithful, as explained above.

Two corollaries follow:
1. Every 1:1 map always reproduces the territory unfaithfully.
2. At the moment the map is realized, the empire becomes unreproducible.

It could be remarked that, with the second corollary, the empire fulfills its own most secret dream, that of making itself imperceptible to enemy empires; but thanks to the first corollary it would become imperceptible to itself as well. We would have to postulate an empire that achieves awareness of itself in a sort of transcendental apperception of its own categorial apparatus in action. But that would require the existence of a map endowed with self-awareness, and such a map (if it were even conceivable) would itself become the empire, while the former empire would cede its power to the map.

Third corollary: every 1:1 map of the empire decrees the end of the empire as such and therefore is the map of a territory that is not an empire.

1982

How
to Eat
Ice Cream

When I was little, children were bought two kinds of ice cream, sold from those white wagons with canopies made of silvery metal: either the two-cent cone or the four-cent ice-cream pie. The two-cent cone was very small, in fact it could fit comfortably into a child's hand, and it was made by taking the ice cream from its container with a special scoop and piling it on the cone. Granny always suggested I eat only a part of the cone, then throw away the pointed end, because it had been touched by the vendor's hand (though that was the best part, nice and crunchy, and it was regularly eaten in secret, after a pretense of discarding it).

The four-cent pie was made by a special little machine, also silvery, which pressed two disks of sweet biscuit against a cylindrical section of ice cream. First you had to thrust your tongue into the gap between the biscuits until it touched the central nucleus of ice cream; then, gradually, you ate the whole thing, the biscuit surfaces softening as they became soaked in creamy nectar. Granny had no advice to give here: in theory the pies had been touched only by the machine; in practice, the vendor had held them in his hand while giving them to us, but it was impossible to isolate the contaminated area.

I was fascinated, however, by some of my peers, whose parents bought them not a four-cent pie but two two-cent cones. These privileged children advanced proudly with one cone in their right hand and one in their left; and expertly moving their head from side to side, they licked first one, then the other. This liturgy seemed to me so sumptuously enviable, that many times I asked to be allowed to celebrate it. In vain. My elders were inflexible: a four-cent ice, yes; but two two-cent ones, absolutely no.

As anyone can see, neither mathematics nor economy nor dietetics justified this refusal. Nor did hygiene, assuming that in due course the tips of both cones were discarded. The pathetic, and obviously mendacious, justification was that a boy concerned with turning his eyes from one cone to the other was more inclined to stumble over stones, steps, or cracks in the pavement. I dimly sensed that there was another secret justification, cruelly pedagogical, but I was unable to grasp it.

Today, citizen and victim of a consumer society, a civilization of excess and waste (which the society of the thirties was not), I realize that those dear and now departed elders were right. Two two-cent cones instead of one at four cents did not signify squandering, economically speaking, but symbolically they surely did. It was for this precise reason, that I yearned for them:

because two ice creams suggested excess. And this was precisely why they were denied me: because they looked indecent, an insult to poverty, a display of fictitious privilege, a boast of wealth. Only spoiled children ate two cones at once, those children who in fairy tales were rightly punished, as Pinocchio was when he rejected the skin and the stalk. And parents who encouraged this weakness, appropriate to little parvenus, were bringing up their children in the foolish theater of "I'd like to but I can't." They were preparing them to turn up at tourist-class check-in with a fake Gucci bag bought from a street peddler on the beach at Rimini.

Nowadays the moralist risks seeming at odds with morality, in a world where the consumer civilization now wants even adults to be spoiled, and promises them always something more, from the wristwatch in the box of detergent to the bonus bangle sheathed, with the magazine it accompanies, in a plastic envelope. Like the parents of those ambidextrous gluttons I so envied, the consumer civilization pretends to give more, but actually gives, for four cents, what is worth four cents. You will throw away the old transistor radio to purchase the new one, that boasts an alarm clock as well, but some inexplicable defect in the mechanism will guarantee that the radio lasts only a year. The new cheap car will have leather seats, double side mirrors adjustable from inside, and a paneled dashboard, but it will not last nearly so long as the glorious old Fiat 500, which, even when it broke down, could be started again with a kick.

The morality of the old days made Spartans of us all, while today's morality wants all of us to be Sybarites.

1989

97

How It Begins, and How It Ends

There is a drama in my life. I pursued my advanced studies as a guest of the University College of Turin, where I had won a scholarship. Of those years I have retained the happiest of memories and a lasting dislike of tuna fish. It so happened that the college refectory remained open for each meal exactly one hour and a half. Those who arrived within the first half hour were served the specialty of the day; latecomers were given tuna. Except for the summer holidays and Sundays, then, over those four years I ate 1920 meals featuring tuna fish. But that is not the drama I refer to.

My drama springs from the fact that, while we students had no money, we still hungered for movies, music, and plays. So we would arrive at the theater ten minutes early and approach the gentleman—what was he called?—the leader of the claque, shaking his hand and slipping a hundred lire into his palm. Then he would admit us. We were a paying claque.

It also happened that the doors of the college were locked inexorably at midnight. After that hour, those who were outside remained out, because there were no residential obligations, and if a student wished, he could be absent even for a month. Practically speaking, this meant that at ten minutes to midnight we had to leave the theater and scurry to our destination. But at ten minutes to midnight the play had not yet ended. And so it was that, over a four-year period, I saw the theatrical masterpieces of every time and place, except for their last ten minutes.

Thus I have lived a lifetime without knowing if Oedipus faced up to the horrible revelation, or what became of the six characters in search of an author, whether Oswald Alving was cured thanks to penicillin, if Hamlet finally discovered that to be was better than not to be. I still don't know who the real Signora Ponza was, if Ruggero Ruggeri/Socrates drank the hemlock, if Othello punched up Iago before setting off on a second honeymoon, if the imaginary invalid's health improved, if everyone threw rice after Romeo and Juliet, and who was Bunbury. I thought I was the only human being afflicted by this ignorance until, casually reliving old memories with my friend Paolo Fabbri, I discovered that for years he has suffered from the same anguish in reverse. During his student years he worked in a theater, organized and run by students; his job was to stand at the door and take tickets. As many ticket-holders arrived late, he was never able to slip into a seat before the beginning of the second act. He saw Lear, blind and raving, wandering around with the corpse of Cordelia in his arms; but he had no idea what had brought the two of them to that ghastly pass. He heard Blanche Dubois profess her faith in strangers, but he racked his brain trying to figure out why such a sweet lady was being carted off to the bin. He never understood why Hamlet was so down on his uncle, who seemed a perfectly nice man. He saw Othello perform his dread act, but had no notion why such a docile little wife was being placed beneath a pillow and not on top of one.

Well, to make a long story short, Paolo and I exchanged confidences. And we discovered that a splendid old age lies before us. Seated on the front steps of a country house or on a bench in the park, for years we will tell each other stories: he, endings; I, beginnings, amid cries of amazement at every discovery of prelude or catharsis.

"You don't mean it! What did he say?"

"He said: 'Mother, I want the sun!'"

"Ah, then he was done for."

"Yes, but what was wrong with him?"

I whisper the answer in his ear.

"My God, what a family! Now I understand . . . ."

"But tell me about Oedipus!"

"There isn't a lot to tell. His Mom commits suicide and he blinds himself."

"The poor kid. All the same . . . they tried to tell him in every possible way."

"True, I just can't figure it. Why didn't he understand?"

"Put yourself in his place. The plague begins. He's a king, happily married . . . ."

"So when he married his Mom, he didn't—"

"Of course not! That's the whole point."

"It's like a Freud case history. If they told you, you wouldn't believe it."

100

Will we be happier afterwards? Or will we have lost the freshness of those who are privileged to experience art as real life, where we enter after the trumps have been played, and we leave without knowing who's going to win or lose the game?

1988

How
to Justify
a Private
Library

Generally speaking, from my childhood on, I have been always subjected to two (and only two) kinds of joke: "You're the one who always answers" and "You resound in valleys." All through my early years I believed that, by some strange chance, all the people I met were stupid. Then, having reached maturity, I was forced to conclude that there are two laws no human being can escape: the first idea that comes into a person's mind will be the most obvious one; and, having had an obvious idea, nobody ever thinks that others may have had the same idea before.

I possess a collection of review headlines, in all the languages of the Indo-European family, going all the way from "The Echo of Eco" to "A Book with Echoes." In the latter case I suspect the printed headline wasn't the first idea that came into the subeditor's mind. What probably happened was this: the editorial staff met, debated some twenty possible titles, and finally the managing editor's face lighted up and he said, "Hey, guys, I've had a fantastic idea!" And the others responded, "Boss, you're a devil! Where do you get them?" "It's a gift," he must have replied.

I'm not saying people are banal. Taking as divine inspiration, as a flash of originality, something that is obvious reveals a certain freshness of spirit, an enthusiasm for life and its unpredictability, a love of ideas—small as they may be. I will always remember my first meeting with that great man Erving Goffman, whom I admired and loved for the genius and penetration with which he could identify infinitesimal aspects of behavior that had previously eluded everyone else. We were sitting at an outdoor café when, looking at the street after a while, he said, "You know something? I believe there are too many automobiles in circulation in our cities." Maybe he had never thought this before because he had had far more important things to think about; he had just had a sudden epiphany and still had the mental freshness to express it. I, a little snob infected by the *Unzeitgemässe Betrachtungen* of Nietzsche, would have hesitated to say it, even if I thought it.

A second shock of banality occurs to many people in my condition—that is, people who possess a fairly sizable library (large enough in my case that someone entering our house can't help but notice it; actually, it takes up the whole place). The visitor enters and says, "What a lot of books! Have you read them all?" At first I thought that the question characterized only people who had scant familiarity with books, people accustomed to seeing a couple of shelves with five paperback mysteries and a children's encyclopaedia, bought in installments. But experience has taught me that the same words can be uttered also by people above suspicion. It could be said that they are still people who consider a bookshelf as a mere storage place for already-read books and do not think of the library as a working tool. But there is more to it than that. I believe that, confronted by a vast array of books, *anyone* will be seized by the anguish of learning, and will inevitably lapse into asking the question that expresses his torment and his remorse.

The problem is that when someone says, "Eco? You're the one who always answers," you can reply with a little laugh and, at most, if you want to be polite, with "That's a good one!" But the question about your books has to be answered, while your jaw stiffens and rivulets of cold sweat trickle down your spine. In the past I adopted a tone of contemptuous sarcasm. "I haven't read any of them; otherwise, why would I keep them here?" But this is a dangerous answer because it invites the obvious follow-up: "And where do you put them after you've read them?" The best answer is the one always used by Roberto Leydi: "And more, dear sir, many more," which freezes the adversary and plunges him into a state of awed admiration. But I find it merciless and angst-generating. Now I have fallen back on the riposte: "No, these are the ones I have to read by the end of the month. I keep the others in my office," a reply that on the one hand suggests a sublime ergonomic strategy, and on the other leads the visitor to hasten the moment of his departure.

1990

104

How
to Compile
an Inventory

The Italian government has given assurances that something will be done to guarantee the autonomy of our country's universities. Italian universities were autonomous in the Middle Ages, and they functioned better than they do today. American universities, whose perfection has become legendary for Europeans, are autonomous. German universities are under the jurisdiction of the regional authorities, but local governments are more alert than a centralized administration, and in many cases—like the appointment of professors—the regional parliament merely ratifies formally what the university itself has already decided. In Italy, if a scientist discovers that phlogiston doesn't exist he will most likely be able to announce his finding only if he happens to teach a course on the Axiomatics of Phlogiston, because a course title, once it is on the ministry's lists, can be changed only after protracted negotiations among all the institutions of higher learning in the country, along with the Superior Council of Education, the Minister, and some other organizations whose names escape me.

Research goes forward because someone glimpses a path that no one has seen before, and a few other people, with exceptional decisional flexibility, decide to believe in him or her. But if someone wants to move a desk in Vitipeno, a decision must come from Rome, after consultations with Chivasso, Terontola, Afragola, Montelepre, and Decimomannu, so obviously the desk will be moved only when the move is no longer necessary.

Teachers engaged on temporary contracts ought to be outside scholars of great reputation and irreplaceable expertise. But between the submission of the university's request and notification of the ministry's approval we usually reach the end of the academic year, with only a few weeks of instruction remaining (unless the ministry simply says no). Clearly, in such an aleatory situation, it is hard to attract a Nobel laureate, and we end up with the dean's unemployed sister-in-law.

Research bogs down also because the bureaucratic routine makes us waste time in solving ridiculous problems. I am the head of a university department. Some years ago we were told to make an inventory of the department's physical possessions, a scrupulous list. Our only available employee was supposed to deal with a thousand other questions. But it was possible to farm out the task to a private organization that asked for three hundred thousand lire. We had the money, but in funds meant for inventoriable materials. How could we declare that an inventory was inventoriable?

I had to set up a committee of logicians, who suspended their own researches for three days. In my statement of the problem they saw something comparable to *The Set of Normal Sets*. Then they decided that the act of compiling an inventory, as it is an act, is not an object and therefore cannot be inventoried, but they further decided that its output is the catalogue of the inventory and, as this is an object, it can be inventoried. We asked the private firm to bill us not for the act but for its result, a result that we then inventoried. For several days I distracted serious scholars from their specific tasks, but I avoided going to jail.

Some months ago the janitors came and told me we were without toilet paper. I told them to buy some. The secretary told me I currently had funds only for inventoriable materials, and pointed out that while toilet paper can be inventoried, the natural tendency of such papers is to vanish, for reasons I prefer not to go into, and once it has vanished, it vanishes also from the inventory. I formed a committee of biologists to ask how we could inventory used toilet paper, and the answer was that such a thing is possible, but at a very high human cost.

I summoned a committee of jurists, who supplied me with the solution. I receive the toilet paper, I inventory it, and I require its distribution among the rest rooms for scientific purposes. If the paper disappears, I report the theft of catalogued material by unknown criminals. Unfortunately, I have to repeat this process every two days, and an inspector from the Secret Services has uttered some heavy insinuations, criticizing an institution that can be infiltrated by unidentified crooks so easily and so frequently. I am under suspicion, but I have an iron-clad alibi. They'll never get me.

The flaw is that to find the solution I had again to remove illustrious men of learning, for days and days, from research that would be of use to our country, while we wasted taxpayers' money on hours of work from teachers and staff, not to mention telephone calls and fax paper. But no one is ever indicted for squandering government money if everything is done within the law.

1986

How
to Spend
Time

When I call the dentist to make an appointment and he tells me that he does not have an hour free at any time in the coming week, I believe him. He is a serious professional. But when someone invites me to a conference, or to a roundtable discussion, or asks me to edit a Festschrift, or write an essay, or join a panel of experts, and I say I haven't time, no one believes me. "Come now, Professor," he says, "a person like yourself can always make time." Obviously we humanists are not considered serious professionals; we are idlers.

I've done some figuring. And I would urge my colleagues with similar occupations to make their own calculations and tell me if I am right. In a normal year (not a leap year) there are 8760 hours. Reckon eight hours' sleep per night, one hour a day to get up, shave, and dress, add a half hour for undressing and setting the glass of water on the commode, and no more than two hours for meals, and we reach a total of 4197.5 hours. Two hours for getting around the city adds another 730 hours annually.

Holding three classes a week, each lasting two hours, and setting aside one afternoon for advising students (100 hours), I spend at the university—in the twenty weeks into which I condense my teaching—220 hours, to which I add 24 hours of exams, 12 hours of examining theses, and 78 hours for faculty meetings and committees. On an average of five theses a year, each averaging 350 pages, each page to be read at least twice, before and after revisions, calculating three minutes per page, I come to 175 hours. For shorter papers, since my assistants deal with many of them, I assume only four for each of our six sessions, averaging thirty pages each: counting five minutes per page what with reading and preliminary discussion; add another 60 hours. Not including my own research, we reach 569 hours in all.

I edit a semiotics review, *VS*, which publishes three numbers yearly, a total of 300 pages. Not counting time spent reading and rejecting manuscripts, ten minutes per page (evaluation, revision, proofs) comes to 50 hours. I direct two series of scholarly volumes pertinent to my field. Six books a year totaling 1800 pages: at ten minutes per page, we have another 300 hours. Translations of my own texts—essays, books, articles, papers read at conferences: considering only the languages I can check, I cover an annual average of 1500 pages at twenty minutes per page (reading, checking against the original, and conferring with the translator, in person, by telephone, or by letter), and that makes 500 hours. Then there are my original writings. Even assuming I do not write a book, essays, papers, reports, notes for lectures, etc. easily amount to 300 pages. If we include time spent thinking, making notes, writing, and revising, at least one hour is spent on each page—another 300 hours. My weekly magazine column, at an optimistic estimate, what with choosing a subject, making notes, consulting a few books, then drafting it, cutting it to the required length, dictating it, and sending it off, takes three hours each week. Multiplying by fifty-two weeks gives 156 hours. (I am not calculating time spent on other, exceptional articles.) Finally, my mail, to which—still leaving much unanswered—I dedicate three mornings a week from nine to one, occupies 624 hours.

I calculate that last year, accepting only ten percent of the proposals received, and limiting myself to conferences closely associated with my discipline, at which I presented my own or my colleagues' research, and various unavoidable appearances (academic ceremonies, meetings required by the relevant ministries), I have totaled 372 hours of active presence (I do not count wasted time). Since many of these engagements were abroad, I calculate 323 hours of travel. This calculation considers that a Milan–Rome trip involves four hours, including taxi to the airport, waiting time, flight, taxi into Rome, settling in at the hotel, and arriving at the meeting place. A trip to New York consumes twelve hours.

It all adds up to 8121.5 hours. Subtracting them from the 8760 hours in a year, I am left with 638.5 hours, in other words about 1 hour 40 minutes per day, which I can devote to sex, conversation with friends and family, funerals, medical care, shopping, sport, theater. As you see, I have not calculated the time spent reading printed matter (books, articles, comics) not part of my work. Assuming I spent my travel time reading, in 323 hours, at five minutes per page (simple reading and annotations), I have had the possibility of reading 3876 pages, corresponding to a mere 12.92 books of 300 pages each. And what about smoking? Sixty cigarettes a day, if each one requires half a minute (finding the pack, lighting up, putting it out), comes to more than 182 hours. Too many. I have to give up smoking.

1988

How
to Buy
Gadgets

The aircraft flies majestically over boundless prairies, immense deserts. This American continent can still offer moments of solitary, almost tactile encounter with nature. I am forgetting civilization, but it so happens that in the pocket of the seat back before me, along with instructions for rapid evacuation (of the plane, in the unlikely event of an emergency), a pamphlet with information about the in-flight movie, and the program of the Brandenburg Concertos available through the headset, there is a copy of *Discoveries*, a brochure that lists, with alluring illustrations, a series of objects that can be purchased via mail order. In the days that follow, on other flights, I discover analogous publications: *The American Traveler*, *Gifts with Personality*, and their similars.

They make irresistible reading, I am won over by them, and I forget nature, so monotonous because, at least here, "non facit saltus" (and I am hoping my aircraft will behave in the same fashion). Culture, as we know, is all the more interesting if it serves to revise and correct nature. Nature is tough and hostile; culture, on the contrary, allows people to do things with less effort, saving time. Culture frees the body from the enslavement of toil and opens the way to contemplation.

Just think, for example, how tedious it is to handle a nasal spray, one of those little pharmaceutical bottles that you press with two fingers to allow a beneficent aerosol to penetrate the nostrils. But relief is at hand! Just insert the bottle into a Viralizer machine ($4.95), and it is squeezed for you, so efficiently that the spray reaches the most intimate areas of the respiratory tract. Naturally, you have to hold the machine in your hand, and the photographs suggest a Kalashnikov being fired, but then everything comes at a price.

I am struck (but I hope not literally shocked) by Omniblanket, which costs all of $150. At the simplest level, it is an electric blanket, but it can be programmed so that the temperature varies from one part of your body to another. In other words, if during the night your back feels cold but your groin tends to sweat, you adjust the program accordingly. Omniblanket will then keep your back warm and your groin cool. If you are nervous and toss and turn in your sleep, ending up with your head at the foot, then you're just out of luck. You will roast your testicles or whatever you have in that area, depending on your sex. I doubt the inventor can be asked to make improvements, because it seems he was burned to a cinder some time ago.

Naturally, in your sleep, you might snore and disturb your partner, if you have one. Well, in that case, try Snorestopper, a kind of watch you fasten onto your wrist before sleeping. The moment you begin to snore the Snorestopper, alerted by an audiosensor, emits an electronic signal that, from your arm, reaches some of your nerve centers and interrupts something or other; anyway, you stop snoring. It costs only $45. One drawback: it is not advisable for those with heart trouble, and I wonder if it might not endanger the health even of an Olympic athlete. Furthermore, it weighs two pounds. You could use it, no doubt, with your husband or wife after decades of familiar intimacy, but hardly with a near-stranger during a night of romance. Making love with a two-pound weight on your wrist could cause alarming side effects.

It is well known that, to reduce their cholesterol levels, the Americans have long since taken up jogging: they run for hours and hours until they drop dead of a heart attack. Pulse-Trainer ($59.95), worn on the wrist, is attached by a wire to a little rubber sheath slipped over the index finger. When your cardiovascular system is on the brink of collapse, an alarm goes off, apparently. A real achievement, if you consider that in underdeveloped countries a person stops running only when he is out of breath—a highly primitive criterion, and perhaps for this reason children in Ghana are not brought up to jog. It is curious, however, that despite such neglect, their blood cholesterol levels are almost imperceptible. With Pulse-Trainer you may run without a care and, further, if you attach to your chest and your waist the two Nike Monitor straps, an electronic voice, programmed by a microprocessor and featuring Doppler-Effect Ultra-Sound, will tell you how many miles you have run and your median speed ($300).

For the animal lover I would advise Bio/Bet. You slip it around your dog's neck and it emits ultrasounds (Pmbc Circuit) that kill fleas. And it costs only $25. I don't know whether, applied to your own body, it would eliminate crabs; I'd be afraid of overkill. Batteries not included. The dog has to go out and buy his own.

Shower Valet ($34.95), a single unit that can be hung on the wall, provides you with a no-mist shaving mirror, integrated radio-TV, and both razor-blade and shaving-cream dispensers. According to the ad, it can transform your boring morning routine into an "experience to remember". Spice Track ($36.95) is an electric machine stocked with little tubes of all the spices you might wish. In poor households the spices are kept in a row on a shelf over the gas stove, and when, for example, the family wants some cinnamon on its daily dish of caviar, they have to sprinkle the spice with their fingers. But, as a member of the privileged class, you will simply tap out an algorithm (in Turbo-Pascal, I believe), and the spice of your choice will come spinning to a stop right in front of you.

If you want to give that special person a present for his or her birthday, a mere thirty dollars is enough to have him/her sent a copy of the *New York Times* of the date of his/her birth. If he/she was born on the day of the dropping of the bomb on Hiroshima, or on the day of the Messina earthquake, that's just too bad. This gift can also be useful in humiliating people you dislike, if they happen to have been born on a day when nothing occurred.

During flights of some length, for three or four dollars, you can hire headsets that allow you to hear various musical programs and the sound track of the in-flight movie. For frequent and compulsive travelers

116

with a pathological fear of AIDS, the sum of $19.95 will buy a personal, or rather personalized (sterilized), headset you can carry with you whenever you fly.

As you move from one country to another, you will want to know how many German marks a British pound is worth, or how many Spanish doubloons you need to buy a thaler. The underprivileged use a pencil or a ten-dollar pocket calculator. They look up the exchange rate in the newspaper and they multiply. But the rich can purchase a twenty-dollar Currency Converter: it gives the same answer as the calculator, but every morning your CEO has to reprogram it according to the newspaper values, and in all likelihood it is unable to answer the (non-monetary) question: what's six times six? The exquisite aspect is that this instrument, costing twice as much, does half what the others can do.

Then there are the various miracle engagement organizers (Master Day Time, Memory Pal, Loose-leaf Timer, etc.). A miracle organizer, superficially, is like an ordinary engagement book (except that as a rule it won't fit into any pocket). As in an ordinary engagement book, for example, after September 30 you find October 1. What changes is the description. Imagine— the helpful example goes—that on January 1 you make an appointment for 10 A.M. on December 20, almost twelve months in the future. No human mind can memorize such an insignificant detail for so long. So what do you do? On January 1, you open the book to the page for December 20 and you write, "10 A.M., Mr. Smith." Wonder of wonders! For most of the rest of the year you can forget that burdensome engagement. And then, at 7 A.M. on December 20, as you are eating your breakfast cereal, you open the book and, as if by

117

miracle, you remember your appointment. . . . But what if on December 20—I ask—you wake up at eleven and don't look at your book until noon? Answer: if you have spent fifty dollars for the miracle organizer, you will at least have the common sense to get up every morning at seven.

To save time at your toilet on that busy December 20 there is the tempting Electric Nose Hair Remover, or Rotary Clipper, for sixteen dollars. This is an instrument that would have fascinated the Marquis de Sade. You stick it into your nose (as a rule) and, as it rotates, it snips off the hairs inside, inaccessible to the nail scissors with which the poor usually, and vainly, attempt to cut them. I haven't been able to find out whether or not there is a macro version for your pet elephant.

Cool Sound is a portable refrigerator for picnics, with built-in TV. The Fish Tie is a necktie in the form of a cod, one hundred percent polyester. The Coin Changer (a little machine that dispenses small change) spares you the trouble of having to dig into your pocket before buying the newspaper: unfortunately, it takes up the space of the reliquary containing St. Alban's femur. There is no information as to where you will find the coins to fill it.

Tea, provided it is of good quality, requires only a vessel for boiling water, a spoon, and, if you like, a strainer. Tea Magic ($9.95) is a highly complicated apparatus that succeeds in making the preparation of a cup of tea as laborious as that of a cup of Turkish coffee.

I suffer from various liver ailments, excess uric acid, atrophic rhinitis, gastritis, housemaid's knee, tennis elbow, avitaminosis, articular and muscular pain,

118

hammertoe, allergic eczemas, and perhaps also leprosy. Fortunately I am not a hypochondriac into the bargain. But the fact is that I must remember every day, at the right time, which pill to take. I have been given a silver pillbox, but I forget to fill it in the morning. Moving around with all those filled bottles means that you must then spend a fortune in leather goods, and it's also inconvenient when you use your skateboard. Now Tablets Cupboard has found the solution to all that. Occupying no more space than a Volvo, it accompanies you throughout your working day and, rotating automatically, it offers you the right pill at the right moment. More elegant, however, is the Electronic Pill Box ($19.85) for patients who have no more than three diseases at any one time. The box has three compartments and a built-in computer that emits a beep at the moment you are to take the pill.

Trap-Ease is magnificent if there are mice in your home. You insert some cheese and set the trap, and then you can even go out to the opera. In a normal trap, the mouse, on entering, touches a spring activating a metal bar that kills him. Trap-Ease, on the contrary, is designed in the shape of an obtuse angle. If the mouse dawdles in the vestibule, he is spared (but he doesn't get to eat the cheese). If he nibbles, the object turns 94 degrees and a shutter comes down. Since the device (which costs eight dollars) is transparent, you can, if you choose, watch the mouse in the evening when there's nothing good on TV; or you can liberate it in the fields (the ecological option), or throw the whole thing in the garbage, or—during sieges— empty the trap directly into a pot of boiling water (or oil).

LeafScoop is a glove that transforms your hands into

those of a palmiped born, through radioactive muta-
tion, from the crossbreeding of a duck with a pterodac-
tyl via Dr. Quatermass. It is used in the collection of
fallen leaves in your eighty-thousand-acre park.
Spending a mere $12.50, you save the salary of a
gardener and a gamekeeper (we recommend it to Lord
Chatterley's attention). TieSaver covers your neckties
with a protective oily film so that, Chez Maxim, you
can eat tomato sandwiches without then appearing at
the Board of Directors meeting looking like Dr. Bar-
nard after a difficult transplant. Only fifteen dollars.
Ideal for those who still use brilliantine. You can wipe
your forehead with the tie.

What happens when your suitcase is crammed to the
bursting point? Fools rush out and buy a second
suitcase, in suede or pigskin. But this solution means
that afterwards you have both hands occupied. Brief-
case Expander is, so to speak, a packsaddle that sits
astride your regular suitcase, and you can use it for
everything that won't fit into the first bag, achieving
an overall girth of six feet or more. For forty-five
dollars you enjoy the sensation of boarding the plane
with a mule under your arm.

Ankle-Valet ($19.95) allows you to conceal your
credit cards in a secret pocket fastened to your calf.
Indispensable for dope smugglers. Drive-Alert is
placed behind the ear when you drive, so that the
moment you doze off—or start to zzz, as the comics put
it—and your head slumps forward beyond an established safety limit, an alarm goes off. The photographs
indicate that it transforms the wearer's ears into
something reminiscent of *Star Trek*, *The Elephant
Man*, or the young Clark Gable. When you are wearing
it, if someone asks you, "Will you marry me?" don't

120

answer with too vigorous an affirmative. The ultra-sounds would do you in at once.

I would also mention in passing an automatic bird-feed distributor, a personalized beer stein with a bicycle bell (ring it to order a second round), a face sauna, a Coca-Cola fountain in the form of a gasoline pump, and Bicycle-Seat: a double bicycle seat, one per buttock. Good for those with a prostate problem. The ad informs us that the device has a "split-end design (no pun intended)."

If between planes you also explore the newsstands, you learn many things. Some days ago I discovered that there are various magazines addressed exclusively to treasure-hunters. *Trésors de l'Histoire*, for example, which is published in Paris, contains articles about fabulous caches possibly buried in various zones of France, giving specific geographical and topographical details and information on treasures already found in those localities.

The issue I bought includes directions regarding treasures to be found even on the bed of the Seine, ranging from ancient coins to objects thrown into the river over the centuries: swords, vases, boats, not to mention other goodies including works of art; there are also treasures buried in Brittany by the apocalyptic sect of Eon de l'Estoile in the Middle Ages; treasures from the magic forest of Brocéliande, dating back to the days of Merlin and the Grail cycle, with detailed instructions for identifying, if you strike it rich, the Holy Grail itself; treasures interred in Normandy by the Vendéens during the French Revolution; the treasure of Olivier le Diable, the barber of Louis XI; treasures mentioned—ostensibly in jest, though they actually exist—in the Arsène Lupin novels. Further, there is a *Guide de la France tréso-raire*, which the article only describes generically, because the complete work is available for 26 francs. It contains 74 maps (scale 1:100), allowing the reader to choose the region most convenient for him.

Meanwhile, the reader will be wondering how you hunt for a treasure underground or underwater. No problem: the magazine offers articles and advertisements describing a vast range of equipment essential for the treasure-hunter. There are different types of detector, variously sensitive to gold or metals or other precious materials. For underwater hunting, there are wetsuits, masks, machines with discriminating devices that identify only jewels, and, of course, there are fins. There are even special credit cards with which, after spending two thousand dollars, you can select another two hundred dollars' worth of goods, free. (The existence of such a bonus is puzzling; by this time the customer should have discovered, at the very least, a casket filled with pieces of eight).

For eight hundred dollars you can be the proud owner of an M-Scan. Though somewhat bulky, it can identify copper coins at a depth of twenty-two centimeters, a chest at two meters, and a metal mass enclosed in an impenetrable cell as much as three meters below your feet. Further instructions explain how to hold and orient the various types of detectors, advising that rainy weather facilitates the hunt for large masses, while dry weather is best for small objects. The Beachcomber 60 is specially engineered for searching beaches and highly mineralized terrain (as you can imagine, if a copper coin is buried next to a vein of diamonds the machine might act up and ignore the coin altogether). Moreover, another ad

122

reminds us that ninety percent of the world's gold is still to be discovered, and the easy-to-handle Goldspear detector (fifteen hundred dollars) has been specially conceived to identify auriferous veins. A pocket detector (Metallocator) is available at a modest price for use in fireplaces and antique furniture. For less than forty dollars, an AF2 spray will clean and remove rust from the coins you find. Also for the less wealthy enthusiast, there are numerous radioesthetic plumblines. And for further information there are numerous volumes with such alluring titles as *The Mysterious Story of French Treasures*; *Guide to Buried Treasure*; *France, the Promised Land*; *Caves and Caverns of France*; and *Treasure-hunting in Belgium and Switzerland*.

You will wonder why, with all this inestimable wealth at their disposal, the editors of this magazine waste the best days of their lives writing instead of setting off for the forests of Brittany. The fact is that the magazine, the books, the detectors, the fins, the rust-cleaners, and all the rest are sold by the same organization, which has a chain of shops virtually covering the continent. So the mystery is quickly elucidated: they have already found their treasure.

What remains to be discovered is the identity of those who enrich these editors, but they are probably the same people who, in Italy, try to find spectacular bargains at televised auctions and rush to exploit the incredible beneficence of wholesale furniture outlets. At least the French enjoy some healthy hikes in the woods.

1986

How to Follow Instructions

Anyone familiar with Italian cafés knows—and has suffered from—those high-tech sugar bowls that are activated by the customer's attempt to remove the spoon from the bowl. At the first, faint tug, the bowl's lid comes down like a guillotine, causing the spoon to fly into the air, scattering sugar throughout the immediate vicinity, while the victim mentally consigns the inventor of this device to a concentration camp. But, on the contrary, that genius is probably enjoying the fruits of his crime on the remote and exclusive beach of some island paradise. The American humorist Shelley Berman once suggested that in the near future the same genius will invent a totally secure automobile, whose doors will open only from the inside.

For a number of years I drove a car that was, in many respects, excellent—except for the fact that the driver's ashtray was set inside the left-hand door. As everyone knows, a driver grips the wheel with his left hand, keeping his right hand free to deal with the gearshift and the various knobs and dials. If you also smoke with your right hand, depositing the ashes in a receptacle to the left of your left shoulder becomes quite a complex operation, one requiring you to remove your eyes from the road ahead. And if the car, like the one I am describing, can attain a speed of eighty miles per hour, the few seconds' distraction it takes to knock ash into the ashtray can mean sodomizing a Mack truck. The gentleman who invented this system was a serious professional who has caused the death of many people, not through tobacco-related cancers, but through collisions with a foreign body.

I have a passion for word-processing systems. If you buy one of these programs, you are given a package with some diskettes, instructions, and a guarantee, which costs anywhere between eight hundred thousand and a million lire. For instruction, you can have recourse either to a company-provided instructor or to the manual. The instructor has usually been trained by the inventor of the sugar bowl mentioned above, and it is advisable to empty a Magnum into his chest the moment he sets foot inside your door. They'll give you perhaps twenty years (less, if you have a smart lawyer), but you will still be saving yourself time.

The real trouble starts when you consult the manual (what I now have to say applies to any manual for any kind of computer program or device). A computer manual appears to be a plastic container with sharp corners, which you must not leave within reach of the children. When you slip the contents out of this container, they seem to be a number of booklets bound in reinforced concrete, and therefore impossible to transport from living room to study. Their titles are conceived in such a way as to prevent you from understanding which should be read first. The less sadistic firms usually give you only two; the more perverse organizations offer as many as four.

Your immediate impression is that the first manual explains things step by step, for the retarded, while the second is addressed to experts, the third to professionals, and so on. Wrong. Each booklet says things that the others do not say; the things you need to know at once are in the manual for engineers, the information for engineers is in the manual for the retarded. Moreover, on the assumption that in future years you will amplify the manual, they are bound in loose-leaf style, with three hundred sheets or more.

Anyone who has handled a loose-leaf notebook knows that, after it has been consulted once or twice, apart from the difficulty in turning the pages, the rings bend out of shape, and soon the binder explodes, shedding leaves all over the room. Human beings accustomed to seek information are used to dealing with objects called books, perhaps featuring pages with color-coded edges or indentations, as in address books, so that readers can promptly find what they need. The authors of computer manuals are unaware of these humane conveniences and supply objects that last about eight hours. The only reasonable solution is to dismember the manuals, study them for six months under the guidance of an Etruscologist, condense them into four file-cards (which will be enough), and throw the originals away.

1985

How
to Become
a Knight
of Malta

I have received a letter on paper headed Ordre Souverain Militaire de Saint-Jean de Jérusalem—Chevaliers de Malte—Prieuré Oecuménique de la Sainte-Trinité-de-Villedieu—Quartier Général de la Vallette—Prieuré de Québec. The letter contains an invitation to become a Knight of Malta. I would have preferred a brief directly from Charlemagne, but I immediately reported the matter to my children, to let them know their father wasn't just any old dad. Then I looked over my shelves for the volume of Caffanjon and Galimard Flavigny, *Ordres et contre-ordres de chevalerie*, Paris, 1982, in which a list of pseudo-orders of Malta is published, circulated by the authentic Sovereign Military and Hospitaler Order of Saint John of Jerusalem, Rhodes, and Malta, whose headquarters is in Rome.

There are another sixteen orders of Malta, all having practically the same name, except for very slight variations; and all repudiate or recognize one another in turn. In 1908 some Russians founded an order in the United States, which in recent years has been headed by His Royal Highness Prince Roberto Paternò II, Ayerbe Aragona, Duke of Perpignan, Head of the Royal Houses of Aragon and the Balearic Islands, Grand Master of the Orders of the Collar of Sant'Agata dei Paternò and of the Royal Crown of the Balearics. But a splinter order broke off from this one in 1934, when a Dane founded a rival order, giving its chancellorship to Prince Peter of Greece and Denmark.

In the 1960s a defector from the Russian branch, Paul de Granier de Cassagnac, founded an order in France, choosing as its protector King Peter II of Yugoslavia. In 1965 the ex-king Peter II of Yugoslavia quarreled with Cassagnac and founded in New York another order whose grand prior, in 1970, was Prince Peter of Greece and Denmark, who then left that order for the Danish one. In 1966 the chancellor of this order was a certain Robert Bassaraba von Brancovan Khgimchiacvili, who was, however, expelled, and who consequently founded the order of the Ecumenical Knights of Malta, whose Imperial and Royal Protector was then to be Prince Enrico III Constantino di Vigo Lascaris Aleramico Paleologo del Monferrato, heir to the throne of Byzantium, Prince of Thessaly, who was later to found yet another order of Malta, the Priorate of the United States, whereas Bassaraba, in 1975, tried to establish his own Priorate of the Trinité de Villedieu, the one to which I would have belonged, but his attempt failed. I then found a Byzantine protectorate, an order created by Prince Carol of Rumania after he broke off from Cassagnac's, a Grand Priorate of which one Tonna-Barthet is the Grand Bailiff, while Prince

Andrew of Yugoslavia—former Grand Master of the order founded by Peter II—is Grand Master of the Priorate of Russia (but then the prince withdrew and the order changed its name to Grand Royal Priorate of Malta and of Europe); an order created in the seventies by a Baron de Choibert and by Vittoria Busa, Orthodox Archbishop Metropolitan of Bialystok, Patriarch of the Western and Eastern Diaspora, President of the Republic of Danzig (*sic*), President of the Democratic Republic of Byelorussia and Grand Khan of Tartary and Mongolia, Viktor Timur II; and an International Grand Priorate created in 1971 by the above-mentioned Royal Highness Roberto Paternò with the Baron-Marquis of Alaro, of which another Paternò became Grand Protector in 1982: head of the Imperial House of Leopardi Tomassini Paternò of Constantinople, heir of the Roman Empire of the East, consecrated legitimate successor of the Apostolic Catholic Orthodox Church of the Byzantine Rite, Marquis of Monteaperto, Count Palatine of the throne of Poland.

In 1971 my order appeared in Malta, born of a schism within that of Bassaraba, under the exalted protection of Alessandro Licastro Grimaldi Lascaris Commenius Vingtmille, Duke of La Chastre, Sovereign Prince and Marquis of Déols, and the Grand Master now is the Marquis Charles Stivala de Flavigny, who after the death of Licastro recruited Pierre Pasleau, who assumes the titles of Licastro as well as those of His Grace the Archbishop Patriarch of the Catholic Orthodox Church of Belgium, Grand Master of the Sovereign Military Order of the Temple of Jerusalem and Grand Master and Hierophant of the Universal Masonic Order of the Ancient Oriental Rite and the Joint Primitive Rite of Memphis and Misraim.

I replaced the volume. Perhaps it, too, contains false information. But I realized that a man has to belong to something, if he doesn't want to feel like nothing. Italy's notorious P2 Lodge has been dissolved, while the Opus Dei has lost all secrecy and is now on everyone's lips. I have made my choice: The Italian Recorder Society. One, True, Ancient, and Accepted.

1986

How
to Deal
with
Telegrams

In the old days, on receiving the mail in the morning, you opened the sealed envelopes and threw away the unsealed ones. Now the organizations that used to send unsealed envelopes send sealed ones, even by special delivery. You open the letter eagerly only to find some absolutely trivial invitation. Especially irritating, because the highest-tech envelopes now have systems of hermetic sealing that resist letter-openers, teeth, jabbing knives. Traditional glue has been replaced by quick-setting cement, the kind dentists use. Luckily we are still safe from promotional schemes, as they always betray themselves with words like "free offer" on the outside, in gold letters. I was taught as a child that when you are offered something free, you should promptly call the police.

But the situation is getting worse. In the past you opened telegrams with real interest, ripping the envelopes in your haste: either they brought some piece of bad news or they informed you of the sudden death of a long-forgotten uncle in America. Now, if someone has a message of no interest to communicate, he sends you a telegram.

Telegrams fall into three categories. The imperative: "You are invited to attend important conference day after tomorrow on cultivation lupins in Apulia Undersecretary Ministry of Forests presiding please telex immediately time of arrival" (then comes a series of acronyms and numbers occupying two pages, in which naturally, and happily, the name of the pretentious sender is lost). The taken-for-granted: "As per previous agreement we confirm your participation conference regarding treatment of paraplegic koalas, please fax immediately." Of course, there was no previous agreement, or perhaps the preliminary invitation is still en route, via ordinary mail. But when the letter does arrive, it has been superseded by the telegram, already discarded, and the letter then follows it into the wastebasket. Finally, there is the third, enigmatic category: "Roundtable on computer science and crocodiles postponed as announced please confirm availability new dates." What dates? What availability? Wastebasket.

Now, however, the telegram has been made obsolete by the invention of overnight express delivery. In this method, which costs sums that would make Tina Brown blanch, the envelope can be opened only with the help of barbed-wire cutters; and once opened, it still does not disclose its contents immediately, thanks to the barrier, composed of various strips of Scotch tape, that must be overcome. Sometimes this system is employed purely for snobbish reasons (like the ceremonies of ritual consumption studied by Mauss); all there is, in the end, is a little note that says "hi" (but hours are spent in hunting for it, because the original envelope is the size of a garbage bag, and not everyone has the long arms of a Mr. Hyde). More often the envelope has a blackmailing function, and also contains a coupon for your reply. The sender is suggesting: "To say what I have to say to you I have spent an outrageous sum of money; the speed of delivery expresses my anxiousness; since there is a prepaid reply, if you don't answer you are a scoundrel." Such arrogance deserves punishment. Nowadays I open only the express envelopes that I myself have asked, by telephone, to be sent to me. The others I throw away, but even then they are a nuisance, because they clog up the basket. I dream of carrier pigeons.

Often telegrams and express envelopes announce awards. In this world there are honors and prizes that everyone is pleased to receive (the Nobel, the Golden Fleece, the Garter, the Irish Sweepstakes) and others that require nothing but acceptance. Anyone who has to publicize a new brand of shoe polish, a retarding condom, or some sulfurous mineral water, organizes an award. It is very easy to get a board of judges together. What's difficult is to find winners. That is to say, they could be found easily if the prizes went to young people at the beginning of their career, but in that case press and TV wouldn't cover the event. So the winner, at the very least, must be Mother Teresa. But if Mother Teresa went to collect all the prizes she is awarded, the death rate in Calcutta would soar. The telegram announcing the prize, therefore, must assume an imperative tone and hint at severe sanctions in the event of refusal: "Happy to inform you that

133

this evening, within one hour, you will be given the Golden Truss stop your presence indispensable in order to receive unanimous vote of unbiased jury otherwise must regretfully honor someone else." The telegram presupposes that the recipient will leap to his feet, screaming, "No, no! It's mine! Mine!"

Oh yes, I almost forgot. There are also those post-cards that arrive from Kuala Lumpur signed "George." George who?

1988

How
Not to
Use the
Fax Machine

The fax machine is truly a great invention. For anyone still unfamiliar with it, the fax works like this: you insert a letter, you dial the number of the addressee, and in the space of a few minutes the letter has reached its destination. And the machine isn't just for letters: it can send drawings, plans, photographs, pages of complicated figures impossible to dictate over the telephone. If the letter is going to Australia, the cost of the transmission is no more than that of an intercontinental call of the same duration. If the letter is being sent from Milan to Saronno, it costs no more than a directly dialed call. And bear in mind that a call from Milan to Paris, in the evening hours, costs about a thousand lire. In a country like ours, where the postal system, by definition, doesn't work, the fax machine solves all your problems. Another thing many people don't know is that you can buy a fax for your bedroom, or a portable version for travel, at a reasonable price. Somewhere between a million five and two million lire. A considerable amount for a toy, but a bargain if your work requires you to correspond with many people in many different cities.

Unfortunately, there is one inexorable law of technology, and it is this: when revolutionary inventions become widely accessible, they cease to be accessible. Technology is inherently democratic, because it promises the same services to all; but it works only if the rich are alone in using it. When the poor also adopt technology, it stops working. A train used to take two hours to go from A to B; then the motor car arrived, which could cover the same distance in one hour. For this reason cars were very expensive. But as soon as the masses could afford to buy them, the roads became jammed, and the trains started to move faster. Consider how absurd it is for the authorities constantly to urge people to use public transport, in the age of the automobile; but with public transport, by consenting not to belong to the elite, you get where you're going before members of the elite do.

In the case of the automobile, before the point of total collapse was reached, many decades went by. The fax machine, more democratic (in fact, it costs much less than a car), achieved collapse in less than a year. At this point it is faster to send something through the mail. Actually, the fax encourages such postal communications. In the old days, if you lived in Medicine Hat, and you had a son in Brisbane, you wrote him once a week and you telephoned him once a month. Now, with the fax, you can send him, in no time, the snapshot of his newborn niece. The temptation is irresistible. Furthermore, the world is inhabited by people, in an ever-increasing number, who want to tell you something that is of no interest to you: how to choose a smarter investment, how to purchase a given object, how to make them happy by sending them a check, how to fulfill yourself completely by taking part in a conference that will improve your professional status. All of these people, the moment they discover you have a fax, and unfortunately there are now fax directories, will trample one another underfoot in their haste to send you, at modest expense, unrequested messages.

As a result, you will approach your fax machine every morning and find it swamped with messages that have accumulated during the night. Naturally, you throw them away without having read them. But suppose someone close to you wants to inform you that you have inherited ten million dollars from an uncle in America, but on condition that you visit a notary before eight o'clock: if the well-meaning friend finds the line busy, you don't receive the information in time. If someone *has* to get in touch with you, then, he has to do so by mail. The fax is becoming the medium of trivial messages, just as the automobile has become the means of slow travel, for those who have time to waste and want to spend long hours in gridlocked traffic, listening to Mozart or Dire Straits.

Finally, the fax introduces a new element into the dynamics of nuisance. Until today, the bore, if he wanted to irritate you, paid (for the phone call, the postage stamp, the taxi to bring him to your doorbell). But now you contribute to the expense, because you're the one who buys the fax paper.

How can you react? I have already had letterhead printed with the warning "Unsolicited faxes are automatically destroyed," but I don't think that's enough. If you want my advice, I'd suggest keeping your fax disconnected. If someone has to send you something, he has to call you first and ask you to connect the machine. Of course, this can overload the telephone line. It would be best for the person who has to send a fax to write you first. Then you can answer, "Send your message via fax Monday at 5.05.27 P.M., Greenwich mean time, when I will connect the machine for precisely four minutes and thirty-six seconds."

1989

How Not to Use the Cellular Phone

It is easy to take cheap shots at the owners of cellular phones. But before doing so, you should determine to which of the five following categories they belong.

First come the handicapped. Even if their handicap is not visible, they are obliged to keep in constant contact with their doctor or the 24-hour medical service. All praise, then, to the technology that has placed this beneficent instrument at their service. Second come those who, for serious professional reasons, are required to be on call in case of emergency (fire chiefs, general practitioners, organ-transplant specialists always awaiting a fresh corpse, or President Bush, because if he is ever unavailable, the world falls into the hands of Quayle). For them the portable phone is a harsh fact of life, endured, but hardly enjoyed. Third, adulterers. Finally, for the first time in their lives, they are able to receive messages from their secret lover without the risk that family members, secretaries, or malicious colleagues will intercept the call. It suffices that the number be known only to him and her (or to him and him, or to her and her: I can't think of any other possible combinations). All three categories listed above are entitled to our respect. Indeed, for the first two we are willing to be disturbed even while dining in a restaurant, or during a funeral; and adulterers are very discreet, as a rule.

Two other categories remain. These, in contrast, spell trouble (for us and for themselves as well). The first comprises those persons who are unable to go anywhere unless they have the possibility of chattering about frivolous matters with the friends and relations they have just left. It is hard to make them understand why they shouldn't do it. And finally, if they cannot resist the compulsion to interact, if they cannot enjoy their moments of solitude and become interested in what they themselves are doing at that moment, if they cannot avoid displaying their vacuity and, indeed, make it their trademark, their emblem, well, the problem must be left to the psychologist. They irk us, but we must understand their terrible inner emptiness, be grateful we are not as they are, and forgive them—without, however, gloating over our own superior natures, and thus yielding to the sins of spiritual pride and lack of charity. Recognize them as your suffering neighbor, and turn the other ear.

In the last category (which includes, on the bottom rung of the social ladder, the purchasers of fake portable phones) are those people who wish to show in public that they are greatly in demand, especially for complex business discussions. Their conversations, which we are obliged to overhear in airports, restaurants, or trains, always involve monetary transactions, missing shipments of metal sections, an unpaid bill for a crate of neckties, and other things that, the speaker believes, are very Rockefellerian.

Now, helping to perpetuate the system of class distinctions is an atrocious mechanism ensuring that, thanks to some atavistic proletarian defect, the nouveau riche, even when he earns enormous sums, won't know how to use a fish knife or will hang a plush monkey in the rear window of his Ferrari or put a San Gennaro on the dashboard of his private jet or (when speaking his native Italian) use English words like "management." Therefore he will not be invited by the Duchesse de Guermantes (and he will rack his brain trying to figure out why not; after all, he has a yacht so long it could almost serve as a bridge across the English Channel.

What these people don't realize is that Rockefeller doesn't need a portable telephone; he has a spacious room full of secretaries so efficient that at the very worst, if his grandfather is dying, the chauffeur comes and whispers something in his ear. The man with power is the man who is not required to answer every call; on the contrary, he is always—as the saying goes—in a meeting. Even at the lowest managerial level, the two symbols of success are a key to the executive washroom and a secretary who asks, "Would you care to leave a message?"

So anyone who flaunts a portable phone as a symbol of power is, on the contrary, announcing to all and sundry his desperate, subaltern position, in which he is obliged to snap to attention, even when making love, if the CEO happens to telephone; he has to pursue creditors day and night to keep his head above water;

and he is persecuted by the bank, even at his daughter's First Holy Communion, because of an overdraft. The fact that he uses, ostentatiously, his cellular phone is proof that he doesn't know these things, and it is the confirmation of his social banishment, beyond appeal.

1991

Three
Owls on
a Chest
of Drawers

The literature on the Italian sestina by the anonymous "Autore della Civetta"[1] now fills a not inconsiderable shelf, so anyone essaying a *Rezeptionsgeschichte* of this brief but significant poem cannot fail, in taking on the mantle of its doxologist, to come up against a certain amount of touchy expertise.

Still, with all due respect to our illustrious predecessors and contemporaries, it may not be without some interest to repeat here the text that has inspired so many different interpretative readings, the nude simulacrum of the *jouissances* that are eluded there, writing and graphos, significant passage, imago, and perhaps phantom.[2]

Let us first consider the text-ture of the definitive version that Segre,[3] with fastidious precision, established as long ago as 1970:

Ambarabà cicci coccò,
tre civette sul comò
che facevano l'amore
con la figlia del dottore.
Ma la mamma le chiamò . . .
Ambarabà cicci coccò.

(literal translation:
Ambarabà cicci coccò,
three snow owls on the chest of drawers
who were making love
with the daughter of the doctor.
But the Mama called them . . .
Ambarabà cicci coccò.)

A certain number of versions of this sestina exist in other languages, *à savoir* the French version produced by the Ouvroir de Littérature Potentielle. It reads as follows:

Ambaraba cici coco,
trois chouettes qui font dodo
en baisant sur la commode
une fille très à la mode.
Mais maman cria aussitôt:
Ambaraba cici coco!

Note the loss of the informative "figlia del dottore" (literally "daughter of the doctor"), restored at the connotative level, however, through the reference to a girl of independent behavior.[4] Then there is an anonymous German version, not without some influence of Hugo Ball and perhaps, to a keen and sensitive ear, an authoritative hint of Christian Morgenstern.

Ambaraba Zi Zi Koko,
Drei Käuze auf dem Vertiko,
Die legten sich aufs Ohr
Mit der Tochter vom Doktor.

Doch da schrie die Mutter so.
Ambaraba Zi Zi Koko!

More interesting in its poetic achievement, though surely *extra moenia* as far as the laws of gender and the complex of extratextual references are concerned, is the translation that the distinguished novelist and scholar Erica Jong attributes to a mysterious Count Palmiro Vicarion.[5]

> There were three old Owls of Storrs
> screwing a Girl on a big Chest of Drawers.
> But the Maid was the Daughter
> of a Doctor, and their Mother
> cried: "Come back, lousy Owls of Storrs!"

Returning to the original, Italian text, we encounter immediately the problem that has so vexed critics: the matter of date. Although the alliteration in the first and last verses prompted Vossler, some time ago, to posit echoes of proto-Latin literature, in particular the *Carmen Fratrum Arvalium*,[6] it is beyond doubt that the sestina cannot date from before the foundation of the University of Bologna, since the girl could then not be described as daughter of a "doctor."[7] It is true, however, as Stanley Fish revealed in his magisterial study[8] of the variants of the poem, that in an early manuscript the third verse does not read "che facevano l'amore" (who were making love) but rather "che facevano l'errore" (who were doing wrong), implying that, rather than making love, they were committing a sin. Thus the sense of love as *crimen* is in no way diminished; if anything, it is reinforced by the subtly moralistic allusion—and thus, as anyone can see, in replacing *errore* by *amore* only in the successive version, the anonymous Author achieved a remarkable paronomasia with the *chiamò* of the fifth verse, creating a metaplastic antithesis (rich in metasemantic results at the level of actantial structures as well) between the anxious, protective love of the mother and the possessive and heedless love of the owls.

Of the owls or, possibly, of the girl: for, as Hobbes and Hobbes[9] have observed, it is not clear whom the mother is calling. It should be obvious that the mother is concerned for her daughter, but in that case—as Allen[10] so perceptively notes—why should she call the owls and not her daughter, unless all family ties, as well as the sexual characteristics of the dramatis personae, are a good deal less obvious than they would appear at a hasty first reading?[11]

In any case, and to return to the problem of date, the poem does not seem to be earlier than the eleventh century A.D., and perhaps it is somewhat later if, as Le Goff suggests, "the chest of drawers appears in the practice and philosophy of interior furnishing with the decline of the feudal economy and with the rise of a peasant class of small landowners, not yet completely free, but in any case liberated from the living conditions of actual serfs. It is toward the seventeenth century, finally, that in the Ardennes there arose the custom of making love on the chest of drawers rather than on straw, not least because the chest of drawers was usually surmounted by a mirror."[12] The virtually primal scene of the owls' love-making, as Marie Bonaparte[13] has pointed out, can of course take place only in a peasant ambience. This observation is an elementary one, as it would be difficult to explain such a concentration of owls in an urban context.

Having thus arrived at an approximate dating of

the sestina, we can examine its strophic and metric structures.

As is obvious at first sight, the poem's opening verse (repeated at the end) consists of two four-syllable units, accented on the first and fourth syllables and on the second and fourth, respectively. This introduces four chiastically arranged lines of catalectic and acatalectic trochaic dimeter; the six verses obey an *abccba* rhyme scheme. A difficult and "splendid achievement," as Scholes[14] observes, when you consider that in an earlier version (of uncertain provenance) the second verse read "tre civette sulla cassettiera" (three owls on the cupboard), with obvious loss of metric and accentual vigor.

In any case, an impressive structural analysis of the sestina can be found in *Les Chouettes*, the masterly study by Jakobson and Lévi-Strauss. The authors take special pains to underline how the first three verses present subhuman entities (the owls and the chest of drawers), while the next three present human beings; and similarly how the second and fourth verses feature subjects while the third and fifth feature actions. This prodigious semantic symmetry is reinforced, with splendid parallelism, by an extraordinary play of phonological oppositions. In the first half of the first (and last) verse the alliteration proceeds via an oral bilabial, lax, grave, voiced, stop, diffuse, whereas in the second half there is an opposition between two pairs of voiceless orsals, in which the first alliterative pair consists of palatalized, strident, compact, diffuse, acute affricates and the second of velar, grave, compact, guttural, tense stops.

This double pseudo-alliteration is paronomastically recalled in the second verse (*ci*vette versus *com*ò), whereas the appearance of the mother represents an elaborate play on the quintuple recurrence of the grave labial nasal (*m*).

At the lexical level, "the owls named in the title of the poem are called by name only once in the text"; further, the labiodental grave constrictive voiced fricative (*v*) of "civette" never recurs in the course of the sestina except in the guise of the labiodental unvoiced grave constrictive fricative (*f*). Thus the presence of the owls, alluded to but never again openly declared, represents in the sestina a *hapax* "that shines like a solitaire." Summoned up also by the anaphoric *che* (third verse)/*le* (fifth verse), the owls still dominate the poem. The birds of Minerva, they are unquestionably a travesty of the "savants austères" and, at the same time, as participants in love-making, of Baudelaire's "amoureux fervents": hence the identification of the beloved maiden with a cat, "orgueil de la maison" since she is exposed on the chest of drawers and "comme eux sédentaire . . . amie de la science [the doctor] et de la volupté [love]." The analysis of Jakobson and Lévi-Strauss does not involve (nor could it have, during that unfortunate period of paleostructuralist severity) the dialectic of desire, which made its triumphant appearance in the critical history of this poem through the justly famous Séminaire XXXV of Jacques Lacan.[15]

As every scholar knows, at the beginning of that seminar *Doctor* Lacan (just whose daughter was the girl on the chest of drawers, anyway?) collected the elephants previously distributed at the end of Séminaire I and distributed among the participants some little owls, asserting that they were more suited to the chest of drawers than the elephants were.[16] Then he noted how, as a rule, a mirror appears above a chest of drawers: but (and here, certainly, we have the stroke of genius in this seminar), while the disciples were concentrating their attention on this most abused paraphernal, Doctor Lacan, with one of his typical coups de théâtre, recognized in the *comò* a typical item of furniture supplied with drawers and then broached his brand-new theory of the *stade du tiroir*.[17]

The drawer is in fact the place of repression, and the poem appeared to Lacan as the very allegory of *Urverdrängung*, whereas the pulsatile action of the owls, only apparently inspired by desire, was revealed as a disguise, not all that implicit, of the *Bemächtigungsstreich*; or rather, as Lacan himself clarified in his limpid French, as an *Überwältigung* of the girl-object.

But it now becomes absolutely necessary to move on to a more viable—and more verifiable—Anglo-Saxon corrective for all this transalpine mist. We must bear in mind that as early as the 1960s, Noam Chomsky,[18] in what he at first defined as Standard Theory of the Chest of Drawers (STCD), had attempted to analyze the WP *ambarabà ciccì coccò* (where WP stands for "What? phrase," from "What?!?" the exclamation of Dwight Bolinger when he was exposed, as native informant, to the utterance of the verse itself). The STCD diagrammed the verse in this fashion:

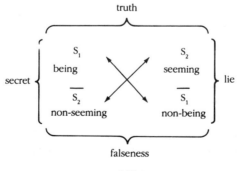

But in the successive phase (Extended Theory of the Owls, ETO), he decided to employ the usual asterisk, labelling the verse as in (1):

(1) *ambarabà ciccì coccò

Truly an *ad hoc* solution, confuted perceptively by Snoopy, Snoopy, and Snoopy (1978) with a reference to Frege, for whom, given that the meaning (in the sense of *Bedeutung*) of every utterance is always a truth-value, and given that all phrases marked by an asterisk are neither true nor false, the meaning of (1) must be considered the equivalent of the meaning of (2):[19]

(2) *Colorless green ideas sleep furiously

But this has the paradoxical result that anyone wishing to make an assertion concerning the *virtus dormitiva* of colorless green ideas should utter (1)—which would in itself be nothing, as Snoopy, Snoopy, and Snoopy observed, were it not for the fact that the owl poem should then be rewritten in these terms:

> (3) Colorless green ideas sleep furiously,
> three owls on a chest of drawers
> were screwing
> the daughter of the doctor.
> But the mother called them,
> colorless green ideas sleep furiously.

While this paradoxical conclusion inspired Harold Bloom to write a probing essay[20] on poetry as misunderstanding, thus furnishing Jacques Derrida the occasion for some provocatory reflections[21] on interpretive drift, the attempt was firmly knocked down by Quine.[22] The last-named observed that, if the utterance (3) had to be read in terms of *post hoc ergo propter hoc* (if the green ideas, etc., *then* three owls, etc.) and if we let

> p = Colorless green ideas sleep furiously
> q = Three owls on the chest of drawers make love with the doctor's daughter

then p could be negated only through *modus tollendo tollens*, namely admitting that q is not true. But since q cannot be negated, given the principle of the identity of indiscernibles, it is impossible to negate p; and thus it must be conceded that colorless green ideas may sleep furiously, which is intuitively false, *salva veritate*.

It is worth remembering the attempt to Chafe, Chafe, and Chafe (1978) whereby *coccò* would be a verb form (third person singular of the preterit of *cocare*) and Ambarabà Ciccì, a proper noun. In this case the sestina should be read as the story of one Ambarabà Ciccì who "coked" three owls on the chest of drawers (the authors did not face the problem of the meaning of *cocare*, as they sustained the legitimacy of a purely distributional analysis). But this hypothesis was famously disproved by Kripke in the light of a causal theory of meaning; it is impossible to identify the expression Ambarabà Ciccì as rigid designator, for want of evidence of an initial baptism.[23]

In response to Searle's objection,[24] namely that Ambarabà Ciccì could be replaced by a definite description, like (4):

(4) The only man who cochoed the owls in Como

Kripke pointed out the problems that would derive from replacing a proper name with a definite description in opaque contexts, as in (5):

(5) John thinks that Nancy hoped that Mary believed that Noam suspected that Ambarabà was not a proper name

For to assert (6)

(6) John thinks that ... the only man who cochoed the owls in Como was not a proper name

is not only without meaning, but patently false, since, as everyone knows,

(7) John is eager to please

and hence John would never venture to invite a general reproach by making such silly assertions.

A vigorous change of direction was imposed on the whole debate by the generative semanticists (see in particular Fillcawley; McJackendoff; Klima-Toshiba and Gulp, 1979). Working with the English version of the poem, they decided to abandon the inconclusive analysis of the first verse to concentrate their attention on the verses that follow, simplified as in (8), for which they devised the accompanying diagram.

(8) Three owls are screwing the girl on the chest of drawers

The stern polemic among transformationalists, generativists, and philosophers of language was finally settled thanks to the intervention of Montague (1977).[25] In an exemplary essay on the poem of the owls, he posited a predicate P

P = being three owls on the chest of drawers who make love with the daughter of the doctor until the mother calls them

whereby the whole poem can be formalized (indexing a possible world w_1):

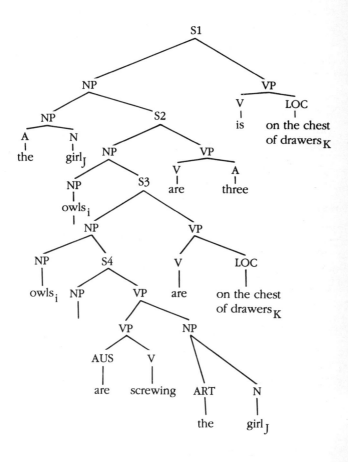

$$P x^{w1}$$

Note that, if we assume that in another possible world, w_2, the predicate P can be stated as:

P = being the sole individual for whom life is a tale told by an idiot

King Lear can properly be represented as:

$$P x^{w2}$$

—which demonstrates almost iconically the profound affinity among all works of art worthy of the name.

But, reacting against the hypersimplification of the Anglo-Saxon schools, Greimas and the Ecole de Paris, after having identified in the poem, as the fundamental level, four actants (Subject, Object, Sender, and Receiver) and having stressed the actorialization implicit in the anthroponyms owl, girl, chest of drawers, and mother, went on to identify two narrative programs: the first $F [S_1 \rightarrow (S_1 \cap O_v)^\circ]$ in which the owls fornicate with the value-object/girl, and the second $F [S_2 \rightarrow (S_1 \cup O_v)]$ in which the mother separates the owls from their object of value. In the course of the first program, given a semiotic square on the order of

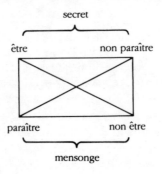

154

the girl (who does not know what the owls are doing to her) seems to play and not play (and is the victim of the owls' lie), while the owls find themselves as the addressees (*destinataires*) of a secret (they make love but do not "seem," and pretend to play doctor with the girl). In the course of the second narrative program the mother discovers the truth and identifies the seeming with the being of the owls. To skip over the intermediary passages of the gripping Greimasian analysis, at its conclusion the author discovers that the profound oppositions of the poem can be depicted on the square as follows:

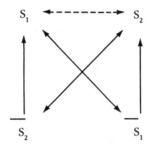

But—and here lies the *punctum dolens* of this otherwise extremely acute study—Greimas in the end no longer knows what to do with the chest of drawers and decides to donate it to the Salvation Army.

The limits of this essay prevent us from considering countless other critical contributions to the fascinating problem of the owls. For the moment we will end by citing the recent essay of Emanuele Severino in which, with a lucid sense of Destiny and with far greater pregnancy and depth than are usually found in the application of the weary methods of every structuralism or formalism, the owls exercising their dominion over the doctor's daughter are seen as the very essence and the vocation of the West.

Only the arrival of the mother thwarts the owls' will to power; so she can be seen as a negation of the nihilism of the essence of the West, a reference to the "second corsair" and the "will of Destiny." But to accept this the owls must necessarily understand that only by renouncing dominion over the world can they comprehend the falsehood of the second utterance, according to which it cannot be true that it is not true that being is nothingness. What is willed is impossible, and the sense of truth is eternally what cannot now or ever succeed in being. Thus the initial *Ambarabà* and the final *Ambarabà* confirm, as scansion of an eternal return, the nothingness of becoming as the irruption of the unheard-of. And the mother only makes evident how predictable the unpredictable was for those who had and cherished a desire to anticipate, *ante-capere*, pre-capture the owls and their defeat. Whence, as at the beginning, always and again *Ambarabà*. The whole is unchangeable.

The chronicler of this critical adventure would like, if he might, to stop at this point, for chronicle is not tautology of the factual, but interrogation and drift; the supreme condition (interrogative arrest) remains that of going forward, and proceeding to return to the origin, and saying not to say, and not saying to be and to remain in the identity of the different. To the point where (the owls have spoken for us, or we for them, and/or the language for all, or silence for the word) no

156

voice will be able to remain silent in the full effability of its own void.

This, and only this, is what Poetry demands of us.

1982

1. T. A. Sebeok, "The Owls and Their Master," in *Zoosebeotics* (Bloomington, Ind.: Donald Duckworth, 1999).

2. Lee Falk and Ray Moore, *The Phantom and the Jungle Owls* (Bandar City, 1936).

3. "Text, Context, Co-Text and Cocotext," in *Textuals* (Texas University Press, 1978).

4. Camille Paglia, "Love on the Chest of Drawers", *Vanity Unfair* 33 (1990).

5. Erica Jong, "Dating a Text," *Frequent Flyers* 3 (1989).

6. Erich Segal, "Historia Noctuae," *Archiv für lateinische allgemeine Kauzwissenschaften* xxxlv, 6 (1960).

7. E. L. Doctorow, *On Doctorowls* (New York: Ragtime Press, 1977).

8. Stanley Fish, *Is There Any Class in This Text?* (Freetext Press, 1991).

9. "Invention of All Mothers," in *Leviathans in Jurassic Park* (London: Owlish Press, n.d.).

10. Woody Allen, *With Feathers* (Manhattan: Getting Even Press, 1992).

11. Leslie Fiedler, *Sex and Owls on the Mississippi* (New Orleans: Huckleberry, 1969).

12. "Temps de la paillasse, temps de la commode," in *Annales* xxx, 1 (1960).

13. In *Edgar Allan Poe, sa vie et son oeuvre*, the author raises the question of what would have happened in "The Raven" if, on the pallid bust of Pallas, three owls had lighted instead of a single raven. Professor Bonaparte subtly observes how difficult it is to make one owl, let alone three, utter "Nevermore" correctly.

14. Robert Scholes, *Protocowls of Reading* (Providence, R. I.: Brown University Press, 1987).

15. For better comprehension I refer to the Urdu translation.

16. It is well known that some Lacanian secessionists insisted on putting elephants on the chest of drawers, bringing about the destruction of a valuable nineteenth-century credenza. This piece had formerly belonged to Little Hans, who, succumbing to the shock, died in a mental hospital in Vienna, in the delusion he was the Man of Wolves.

17. "La parole dont je me leurre ne pourra que se taire dans l'éclatement de ce qu'elle cache. Et pourtant . . . ." One hundred eighty minutes of silence followed while Dr. Lagache tried to extricate himself from a Borromeo knot, yelping constantly (cf. Julia Kristeva, "Chora-Chora!", in *Tell Quayle* 5 (1980), from page 70 to 22.

18. According to Richard Rorty (*Philosophy and the Mirror on a Chest of Drawers*, New York: Owlish Press, 1990) in the last phase of his thinking, Lacan considered continuing the experimental placing of a pocket mirror on a cigar box, since in the bankruptcy of the Ecole Freudienne his chest of drawers had been confiscated.

19. Jeffrey Nurnberg, *Personal Communication* (forthcoming).

20. "Misunderstanding Kabbalah," in *Journal of Aesthetics* 666, iii, n.d. As a typical example of misunderstanding see Allen Ginsberg, *Howl* [*sic*] (San Francisco: City Lights Books, 1956).

21. Jacques Derrida, "Limited Ink" (unfinished paper).

22. "Too Many Owls in Elm Street," in *Gavagai* 5 (1981). In the same issue see also Hilary Putnam, "Owls in a vat," as well as Marvin Minsky, "A Society of Minks." For the whole debate see Daniel Dennett, *Putnaming Owls* (Kuhnisberg: Bestsellers Press, 1979).

23. "Ambarabà in S5," in *Splash! Journal of Rigid Designation*, n.p., n.d.

24. John Searle, "The Owl Is in the Bowl," in *Cats & Mats* 2

(1987). Both Kripke and Searle had obviously been misled, perhaps by a defective critical edition. In fact they read *comò* as *Como* (toponym) and inevitably their interpretation of the poem was contaminated. Obfuscated by the conviction that the owls were in Como, Kripke limited his research on the baptismal rite to the parish records of Como. This would explain his (wrong) conclusion that no Ambarabà Ciccì ever existed, whereas it would be correct to assert that no Ambarabà Ciccì ever existed in Como—nothing excluding the possibility that he (or she) is alive and well in Mexico City.

25. It is well known that Montague abandoned his fruitful research on the owls since he was later fascinated by speaking horses. See for instance (in *Formal Philosophy*, New Haven and London: Yale University Press, 1974: 242): "*Jones seeks a horse such that it speaks* and *a horse such that it speaks is a(n) entity such that Jones finds it* are in DS_{L_1}, but neither K_1-entails the other in L_1."

Editorial
Revision

These days, especially in the United States, implacable copy editors demand of authors not only stylistic revisions but even changes in plot, new endings, whatever commercial necessity dictates. But when we Italians recall—for example, the summary way the novelist-editor Elio Vittorini dealt with young writers some decades ago, can we honestly say that they ordered things so differently in the past?

Take the usually overlooked fact that the first version of a well-known poem by Philip Larkin originally went: "They do you harm, your father and mother." It was only the insistence of Larkin's editor that inspired the now-famous variant. And the first draft of Eliot's *Waste Land* opened: "April is the cruellest month. And March isn't all that great, either." Weakened in its impact by this peevish insistence on climatic details, the earlier text denied April any implied link with the rites of vegetation. As everyone knows, Ariosto at first submitted to his publisher a very brief poem that went: "Of women and knights, arms, loves, courtly rituals, and bold ventures I have nothing to say." And that was that. "How about developing it a bit?" the editor suggested. And Messer Ludovico, who was having enough trouble as civil governor of a remote Tuscan province, said, "What's the use? There are dozens of epics of chivalry already. Leave it. I want to urge poets to try new genres." And the editor replied, "Yes, of course, I understand, and, personally, I agree with you. But why not try approaching the form from another angle? With irony, for instance. Anyway, we can't sell a one-page book, particularly one with only two verses on the page. It looks like imitation Mallarmé. It would have to be a limited, numbered edition. So unless we can get Philip Morris to sponsor it, we're screwed."

The Manzoni case is important. He began the first version of his novel with "That stretch of Lake Garda." It seems simple enough, but if he had stuck to that lake, he might have written the whole history of the Venetian Republic and never got beyond Riva. You can imagine how long it would have taken Renzo to get to Milan. He'd never have made it in time for the bread riot. And afterwards nothing significant would have happened to the poor youth. Lucia would have sought protection from the Nun of Rovereto, an abbess of impeccable behavior; the whole novel would have ended after a few trivial mishaps before the happy wedding. . . . Even Brother Cadfael has more exciting adventures.

The Leopardi story is still more serious. The wandering shepherd of Asia, in the first draft, cried: "What are you doing, Jupiter, in heaven? Tell me, what are you doing, silent Jupiter." Nothing wrong with that excellent planet, of course, but it is visible only during certain seasons and has hardly any emotional or metaphysical connotations. In fact, Leopardi's composition consisted of just a few verses, at the end of which the shepherd concluded that, as far as he was concerned, Jupiter didn't amount to much. Luckily, the editor's intervention saved the day: "Professor Leopardi, give me a break! Use the old imagination. Why not try one of Jupiter's satellites?" "Oh, please! . . . that would only make things worse. What would a wandering shepherd of Asia know about satellites? Maybe the moon . . . at most. You want me to have him cry out to the moon? Really! I do have some self-respect." "Well, you never know. Run it through the machine."

The Proust story, finally, is tragic. In the first version he had written: "Longtemps je me suis couché après minuit." You know what happens to a growing boy who stays up till all hours. The Narrator succumbed to a cerebral inflammation that virtually destroyed his memory. He saw the Duchesse de Guermantes the next day and asked, "Who are you, Madame?" He was banished from all the salons of Paris, because certain faux pas are beyond forgiveness in that world. In this Ur-version, the Narrator was even incapable of expressing himself in the first person, and *La Recherche* boiled down to a brief case history à la Charcot.

On the other hand, after I ended a novel of mine with the verse of Bernard de Morlay beginning, "Stat rosa pristina nomine," I was informed by some philologists that certain other extant manuscripts read, on the contrary, "Stat Roma," which, for that matter, would make more sense because the preceding verses refer to the disappearance of Babylon. What would have happened if I had in consequence entitled my novel *The Name of Rome*? I would have had a preface by John Paul II, who no doubt would have made me a Papal Count. Or someone would have made a movie with Sean Connery in a toga.

1990

Sequels

In 1991 the Italian novelist Laura Grimaldi wrote a Monsieur Bovary, *recounting what happened to Charles after Emma's death; and at about the same time, a Ms. Ripley (probably a character invented by Patricia Highsmith) made a killing with her* Scarlett, *a continuation of* Gone with the Wind. *For that matter, from* Oedipus at Colonus *to* Twenty Years After, *the tradition of the sequel has earned a certain nobility.*

Giampaolo Proni, with his The Case of the Asia Computer, *showed that he knows how to invent narrating machines; and he suggested that I offer some other possible continuations of famous novels.*

Marcel who?

Proust's Narrator, having concluded his work with the seal of Time, exhausted by asthma, decides to visit a celebrated allergy specialist on the French Riviera and travels there by motorcar. An inexperienced driver, he is involved in a frightful accident: severe concussion, almost total loss of memory. He is treated by Aleksandr Luria, who advises him to develop the technique of the interior monologue. Since the Narrator no longer has a store of memories to monologue about and can barely assimilate his present perceptions, Luria suggests he extend the interior monologues in Joyce's *Ulysses*.

The Narrator struggles through the unbearable novel, and reconstructs a fictitious ego for himself, beginning with the memory of his grandmother's visits to him in boarding school at Clongowes Wood. He regains a fine synesthetic ability, and the slightest whiff of mutton fat from a shepherd's pie brings to his mind the trees of Phoenix Park and the spire of the church at Chapelizod. He dies, a Guinness addict, in a doorway on Eccles Street.

Molly

Waking from a troubled sleep on the morning of June 17, 1904, Molly Bloom goes down to the kitchen and finds Stephen Dedalus there, making himself some coffee. Leopold has gone out on one of his vague business errands; perhaps he has deliberately left the two alone. Molly's face is puffy from sleep, but Stephen is immediately fascinated, seeing her as a kind of wondrous whale-woman. He recites some cheap poems to her and Molly falls into his arms. They run away together to Pula, on the Istrian coast, and then to Trieste, with Bloom pursuing them the whole time, disguised as the man in the mackintosh.

In Trieste, Italo Svevo advises Stephen to write down his story, and Molly, who is very ambitious, chimes in.

Over the years, Stephen writes a monumental novel, *Telemachus*. When he has completed the last page, he abandons the manuscript on his desk and elopes with Sylvia Beach. Molly discovers the manuscript, reads it, and becomes completely engrossed in it, finding herself back at the exact point where everything started, stirring restlessly in her bed in Dublin, on the night between June 16 and 17, 1904.

Crazed with rage, she follows Stephen to Paris. At the door of Shakespeare & Co., rue de l'Odéon, she offs him with three pistol shots, shouting "Yes, yes, yes!" She then takes flight, accidentally entering a comic strip by Daniele Panebarco, where she discovers Bloom in her bed making love with—simultaneously—Anna Livia Plurabelle, Lenin, Sam Spade, and Barbara Walters. Distraught, she kills herself.

Sam again

Vienna, 1950. Twenty years have passed, but Sam Spade is still determined to get hold of the Maltese falcon. His current connection is Harry Lime, and the two of them are confabulating at the top of the Prater's Ferris wheel. "I've found a clue," Lime says. Descending, they head for the Café Mozart, where, in one corner, a black musician is playing *As Time Goes By* on a zither. At the little table in the rear, a cigarette in the corner of his mouth, which is wearing a bitter smile, there is Rick. Among the documents Ugarte showed him, he has found a clue; he shows Sam Spade a photograph of Ugarte. "Cairo!" the private eye murmurs. "When I knew him he went by the name of Peter Lorre," Lime says with a sneer.

Rick continues: in Paris, which he entered in

triumph with de Gaulle and his forces, he learned of the existence of an American spy, whom the OSS had released from San Quentin in order to set him on the trail of the falcon. The word then was that he had killed Victor Laszlo in Lisbon. He should be arriving any minute. The door opens and a woman appears. "Ilsa!" cries Rick. "Brigid!" cries Sam Spade. "Anna Schmidt!" cries Lime. "Miz Scarlett!" the black man cries, turning that gray color that blacks turn when they blanch, "You're back! Don't hurt Massa!" The woman has an enigmatic smile. "I am as you desire me. . . . And as for the falcon . . ."

"Yes?" the others all cry, in one voice.

"As for the falcon," the fascinating adventuress replies, "it wasn't a falcon. It was a hawk."

"Screwed!" Spade murmurs, "and for the second time!" He clenches his jaw, making his profile all the more sharp.

"Give me back that hundred dollars," Harry Lime says. "You never get anything right."

"A cognac," Rick orders, ashen.

From the end of the bar the form of the man in the mackintosh emerges, a sarcastic smile playing about his lips. It is Captain Renault. "Come, Molly," he says to the woman. "The Deuxième Bureau men are waiting for us at Combray."

1982

How
to Use
Suspension
Points

In "How to Recognize a Porn Movie" we saw that to distinguish a pornographic film from a film that merely depicts erotic events, it is sufficient to discover whether, to go from one place to another by car, the characters take more time than the spectator would like or the story would require. A similar scientific criterion can be applied to distinguish the professional writer from the Sunday, or non-writer, (who can still be famous). This is the use of suspension points in the middle of a sentence.

Writers use suspension points only at the end of a sentence, to indicate that more could be written on the subject ("and this point could be further elaborated, but . . ."), or, in the middle of a sentence or between two sentences, to underline the fragmentary nature of a quotation ("Friends . . . I come to bury Caesar . . ."). Non-writers use these dots to crave indulgence for a rhetorical figure that they consider perhaps too bold: "He was raging like a . . . bull."

A writer is someone determined to extend language beyond its boundaries, and he therefore assumes full responsibility for a metaphor, even a daring one: "The moving waters at their priestlike task/Of pure ablution round earth's human shores." Everyone agrees that Keats has allowed his fancy to soar, but at least he makes no apology for that. The non-writer, on the other hand, would have written: "The moving waters at their . . . priestlike . . . task/Of pure . . . ablution." As if to say: don't mind me, I'm only joking.

A writer writes for writers, a non-writer writes for his next-door neighbor or for the manager of the local bank branch, and he fears (often mistakenly) that they would not understand or, in any case, would not forgive his boldness. He uses the dots as a visa: he wants to make a revolution, but with police permission.

The following little list of variations may serve to indicate the ghastliness of these dots, suggesting what might have happened to literature if our writers had lacked self-confidence:

"A . . . rose by any other name."

"Never send to know . . . for whom the bell . . . tolls."

"A man's a . . . man for a' that."

"Call me . . . Ishmael."

"The widow Douglas she took me for her . . . son, and allowed she would sivilize me."

"Who's afraid of . . . Virginia Woolf?"

"April is the cruellest . . . month."

"I am a camera with its . . . shutter open."

And so, down to: "riverrun, past Eve and . . . Adam's."

Not that it matters if the Great would have looked

foolish. But, as you see, these dots, suggesting the writer's fear of using bold, figured speech, can also be used to suggest his suspicion that the rhetorical figure, by itself, will seem literal and flat. An example. The *Communist Manifesto* of 1848 begins, as everyone knows, with the words "A specter is haunting Europe," and you must admit this is a great incipit. It would still be pretty good if Marx and Engels had written "A ... specter is haunting Europe"; they would merely have suggested, perhaps, that communism might not be such a terrible and elusive thing, and the Russian revolution might have taken place fifty years earlier, maybe with the Czar's consent, and Mazzini would have taken part in it, too.

But what if they had written "A specter is ... haunting Europe"? Is there some doubt about its haunting? Is it stable? Or do specters, per se, appear and disappear in a flash, suddenly, with no real time for haunting? But that isn't all. What if they had written "A specter is haunting ... Europe"? Would they have implied that they were really exaggerating, that the specter at most might be haunting Trier, and people everywhere else needn't worry? Or would they be suggesting that the specter of communism was already haunting also the Americas and—who could say?—maybe even Australia?

"To be or ... not to be, that is the question." "To be or not to be, that is the ... question." "To be or not ... to be, that is the question." You can see how much work Shakespearean scholarship would have to do, plumbing the Bard's meanings.

All men are created equal.

All ... men are created equal.

All men are ... created equal.

All men are created . . . equal.

All men are created equally entitled to use suspension points.

1991

How
to Write
an Introduction

The purpose of this article is to explain how you put together the introduction to a book of essays, a philosophical treatise, or a collection of scientific articles, to be published, ideally, by a university press or its equivalent, all in accordance with the rules long established in the academic world.

In the paragraphs that follow I will clarify, as succinctly as possible, why an introduction must be written, what it must comprise, and how to list the acknowledgments: for skill in making acknowledgments is the hallmark of the thoroughbred scholar. It can sometimes happen that a scholar, his task completed, discovers that he has no one to thank. Never mind. He will invent some debts. Research without indebtedness is suspect, and somebody must always, somehow, be thanked.

In preparing this article I have drawn on a long and invaluable familiarity with scholarly publications; these have been brought to my attentin by the Ministry of Public Education of the Italian Republic, the Universities of Turin and Florence, the Polytechnic Institute of Milan, and the University of Bologna, as well as New York University, Yale University, and Columbia University.

I could not have completed this work without the patient and impeccable collaboration of Signora Sabina, thanks to whom my study, which by 2 A.M. is reduced to an undefined mass of cigarette stubs and waste paper, every morning is found in acceptable condition once more. My special thanks also to Barbara, Simona, and Gabriella, whose efforts have saved my hours of reflection from the importune interruption of transatlantic calls inviting me to conferences on the most disparate subjects, alike only in being remote from my personal interests.

This article would not have been possible without the unfailing assistance of my wife, who, always ready with the reassurance that all is vanity, was—and is— able to tolerate the moods and demands of a scholar constantly obsessed by the major problems of existence. Her devotion in offering me apple juice, successfully passing it off as the most refined Scotch malt, has been an immeasurable and incredible contribution, documented by the fact that these pages have retained a minimum of lucidity.

My children have been a source of great comfort to me and have provided me with the affection, the energy, and the confidence to complete my self-imposed task. Thanks to their complete, Olympian detachment from my work, I have found the strength to conclude this article after a daily struggle with the definition of the intellectual's role in a postmodern society. I am indebted to them for inspiring an unshakable determination to withdraw into my study and write these pages, rather than encounter in the hall their best friends, whose hairdresser follows esthetic criteria that revolt my sensibilities.

The publication of this text has been made possible by the generosity and the economic support of Carlo Caracciolo, Lio Rubini, Eugenio Scalfari, Livio Zanetti, Marco Benedetto, and the other members of the board of directors of the publishing firm of *L'Espresso*. My special thanks to the business manager, Milvia Fiorani, whose continuing monthly assistance has allowed my research to go forward. That countless readers will hold this modest contribution in their hands is due to the director of the distributing services, Guido Ferrantelli.

Creation and revision of this text have been encouraged by Olivetti, which provided me with an M 21 computer. I would like to express my gratitude for the MicroPro and its Wordstar 2000 program as well. The text has been printed on an Okidata Microline 182.

I could not have made the lines above and below available to the English-language audience without the affectionate, constant insistence and encouragement of Grace Budd, Otello Venturovic, Michael Kandel, Martha Browne, and Dr. Ferdinando Adornato, who have sustained me with heart-warming and pressing daily telephone calls, informing me that the presses were rolling and that, at all costs, I had to provide the final footnotes.

Obviously, they are in no way accountable for the

scholarly content of what appears on these pages; any defects in the present article, as in those of the past and the future, are my responsibility alone.

1987

How
to Write
an Introduction
to an Art
Catalogue

The following notes are meant to assist writers of
introductions to art catalogues (hereafter referred to
as WIAC). But first a word of warning: these instructions are not valid for the writing of a critical-histori-
cal essay to be published in a scholarly review. There
are numerous, complex reasons for this distinction, the
first of which is that critical essays are read and judged
by other critics and only rarely by the analyzed artist,
who either does not subscribe to the publication or has
been dead for two centuries. A catalogue for a show of
contemporary art exists in quite a different context.

How does one become a WIAC? Unfortunately, the
process is all too easy. You have only to be involved in
some intellectual profession (nuclear physicists and
molecular biologists are in great demand), have a
listed telephone number, and enjoy a certain fame.
Fame is calculated in this fashion: it must have a

geographical extension superior to the impact area of the show (fame should be at state level for a city of less than seventy thousand inhabitants, at national level for a state capital, at worldwide level for the capital city of an independent nation, San Marino and Andorra excepted) and must be of a depth inferior to that of the cultural knowledge of possible purchasers of pictures (if the show features wooded landscapes in the style of Daubigny, it is not necessary—indeed, it is counterproductive—for the writer to be a contributor to *The New York Review of Books*; it would be more advisable for him to be the principal of the local teachers' college). Naturally, you must be invited by the exhibiting artist, but this is not a problem: exhibiting artists far outnumber potential WIACs. Given these conditions, your engagement as WIAC is inevitable, quite independent of your will. If the artist has made up his mind, the potential WIAC cannot escape the task, unless he decides to emigrate to another continent.

Now, when the WIAC has accepted, he can decide on one of the following motivations:

1) Corruption (very rare, for, as we shall see, there are motivations that cost the artist less). 2) Sexual reward. 3) Friendship, in either of its two versions: genuine affection or inability to refuse. 4) Gift of a work by the artist (this motive is not the same as the following one, namely admiration for the artist; in fact, it is possible to want gifts of pictures in order to accumulate a commercially viable stock). 5) Sincere admiration for the artist's work. 6) Desire to link one's own name with the name of the artist: a splendid investment for young intellectuals, since the artist will go to great pains to publicize the WIAC's name in

bibliographies for innumerable later catalogues, both nationally and abroad. 7) Ideological, aesthetic, or commercial association, to promote a political movement or assist an idealistic art gallery.

The latter raises a delicate question, which even the most resolutely altruistic WIAC cannot evade. In fact, literary, film, or theater critics, whether they praise or demolish the work they criticize, have fairly little effect on its fate. The literary critic, with a favorable review, may increase a novel's sales by a few hundred copies; the movie critic can pan a cheap porno comedy without preventing it from taking in vast sums at the box office, and the same observation applies to the drama critic. The WIAC, on the other hand, contributes to the enhancement of all the artist's work, occasionally causing its value to jump by a factor of ten.

This special position also affects the critical situation of the WIAC: while the literary critic can speak ill of an author he may or may not know, but who as a rule cannot control the appearance of the article in a given paper, the artist commissions and controls his catalogue. Even when he says to the WIAC, "Feel free to be severe," the situation is, in point of fact, untenable. Either you refuse—but as we have seen, this is impossible—or you are, at the very least, polite. Or evasive.

This is why, since the WIAC wants to maintain his dignity and his friendship with the artist, evasiveness is the essential element in art catalogues.

Let us examine an imaginary situation. We'll take the painter Prosciuttini, who for thirty years has been painting ochre backgrounds with, in their center, a superimposed blue isosceles triangle, its base parallel to the southern edge of the painting. Over it is a red scalene triangle, tilted to the southeast with respect to the base of the blue triangle. The WIAC must bear in mind the fact that, depending on the period in the painter's development, the artist will have entitled his painting, in this order from 1950 to 1980: *Composition*, *Two plus Infinity*, *Minimal*, *Make Love not War*, *Watergate*, *Effete Snobs*, *A/cross*, *Miss/reading*, *Pictorially Correct*. What (honorable) possibilities does the WIAC have, in writing his contribution? If he's a poet, it's easy: he dedicates a poem to Prosciuttini. For example: "Like an arrow—(Ah! cruel Zeno!)—the flash—of another dart—parasang traced—on a cosmos infected—with black holes—of every color!" This solution creates new prestige—for the WIAC, for Prosciuttini, for the dealer, for the purchaser.

The second solution is for writers of fiction only, and it takes the form of a freewheeling open letter: "Dear Prosciuttini, When I look at your triangles, I am once more at Uqbar, with Jorge Luis ... A Pierre Menard who suggests forms recreated in another era, a Don Pitágoras de la Mancha. Lust at 180 degrees: can we rid ourselves of Necessity? It was a June morning, in the sun-baked countryside: a hanged partisan from a telegraph pole. In adolescence, I doubted the substance of the Rule. ..." Et cetera.

If the WIAC has a scientific background his task is much easier. He can begin with the conviction (correct, as it happens) that a picture, too, is an element of Reality; then all he has to do is talk about the profundities of reality and, no matter what he says, he will not be lying. For example: "Prosciuttini's triangles are graphs. Propositional functions of concrete typologies. Knots. How to proceed from knot U to another knot?

As everyone knows, an evaluating function F is required, and if, for every other knot V considered, F (U) appears less than or equal to F (V), it is necessary to "develop" U, in the sense of generating knots that descend from U. A perfect function of evaluation will then fulfill the condition F (U) less than or equal to F (V), so that D (U,Q) is then inferior or equal to D (V,Q), where (obviously) D (A,B) is the distance between A and B in the graph. Art is mathematics. This is what Prosciuttini is telling us."

At first sight this tactic might seem to work well for an abstract painting but not for a Morandi or a Norman Rockwell. Wrong. Naturally everything depends on the skill of the man of science. As a generic indication, we would say that, today, adopting—with a fair amount of metaphorical nonchalance—René Thom's theory of catastrophes, we can demonstrate that Morandi's still lifes represent forms on that extreme edge of equilibrium beyond which the natural forms of the bottles would become cusps beyond and against themselves, cracking like a crystal injured by an ultrasonic sound; the painter's magic thus consists in the very fact of having depicted this extreme situation. The writer could also play with the meaning of the words: *still*, i.e., for a temporal extension—but until when? Magic of the difference between still living and living on.

Another possibility existed from 1968 until, roughly, 1972: the political interpretation. Observations on the class struggle, on the corruption of objects tainted by their commodification. Art as rebellion against the world of consumer goods, the triangles of Prosciuttini as forms that refuse to become trade values, open to working-class inventiveness, expropriated by capitalistic greed. The return to a golden age, announcement of a utopia.

All that has been said so far, however, applies only to the WIAC who is not a professional art critic. The art critic's situation is, shall we say, more critical. He must somehow talk about the work, but without expressing any value judgments. The easiest solution is to show that the artist has worked in harmony with the dominant view of the world or, as we say now, the Influent Metaphysic. Any sort of metaphysic represents a way of accounting for what is. A picture undoubtedly belongs in the category of things that are and, moreover, no matter how bad it may be, it somehow represents that which is (even an abstract painting represents that which could be, or that which is in the universe of pure forms). If, for example, the Influent Metaphysic sustains that everything that is is nothing but energy, to say that Prosciuttini's painting is energy and depicts energy is not a lie: at worst, it is obvious, but obvious in a way that saves the critic, while making Prosciuttini happy, not to mention his dealer, and the possible purchaser.

The problem is to identify that Influent Metaphysic of which, because of its popularity at a given time, everybody has heard. To be sure, you can join Berkeley is asserting that *esse est percipi* and say that Prosciuttini's works are because they are perceived: but as the metaphysic in question is not particularly influent, both Prosciuttini and the readers of the catalogue would perceive the excessive obviousness of the statement.

Therefore, if Prosciuttini's triangles had had to be described in the late fifties, exploiting the Sartre–Merleau-Ponty influence (and, above all, the teachings of Husserl), it would have been suitable to define the triangles in question as "the representation of the very act of intending, which, setting up eidetic regions, turns those same pure forms of geometry into a modality of the Lebenswelt." In that period, too (as variations were permissible also in terms of the psychology of form), to say that Prosciuttini's triangles have a "gestaltic" pregnancy would have been unassailable—*every* triangle, if it is recognizable as a triangle, has a gestaltic pregnancy. In the sixties, Prosciuttini would have seemed more à la page if in his triangles a structure homologous to Lévi-Strauss's parental patterns could be discerned. Desiring to play with structuralism in '68, the WIAC could have said that, according to Mao's theory of contradiction, which subsumes the Hegelian triad in the binary principles of yin and yang, the two triangles of Prosciuttini evidenced the rapport between primary contradiction and secondary contradiction. It must not be thought that the structuralist module could not also be applied to Morandi: deep bottle as opposed to surface bottle.

After the sixties the critic's options became freer. Naturally, the blue triangle intersected by the red triangle is the epiphany of a Desire in pursuit of an Other with which it can never identify itself. Prosciuttini is the painter of Difference, or rather of Difference within Identity. Difference within Identity is also found in the "heads/tails" relationship of a hundred-lira coin, but Prosciuttini's triangles would lend themselves also to pinpointing a case of Implosion as, for that matter, would the paintings of Pollock or the introduction of suppositories into the anal tract (black holes). In Prosciuttini's triangles, however, there is also the reciprocal cancellation of use value and exchange value.

With astute reference to Difference in the smile of the Mona Lisa, which, seen obliquely, can be recognized as a vulva, and is in any case *béance*, Prosciuttini's triangles, with their reciprocal cancellation and "catastrophic" rotation, could appear as an implosiveness of the phallus that becomes cogged vagina. The phallus of Fallacy. In other words, to conclude, the golden rule for the WIAC is to describe the work is such a way that the description, besides being applicable to other pictures, can be applied also to the emotional experience of looking in a delicatessen window. If the WIAC writes, "In Prosciuttini's paintings perception of forms is never inert reception of sense-data. Prosciuttini tells us that there is no perception without interpretation and work, and the passage from the felt to the perceived is activity, praxis, being-in-the-world as construction of Abschaltungen cut deliberately in the very flesh of the thing-in-itself," the reader recognizes Prosciuttini's truth because it corresponds to the mechanisms through which he distinguishes, in the deli, a slice of baloney from the macaroni salad.

Which establishes, in addition to a criterion of viability and efficacy, also a criterion of morality: it is enough to tell the truth. Naturally, truth comes in all sizes.

1980

Appendix

The following text was actually written—by me—to introduce the painting of Antonio Fomez in accordance with the rules of post-modern quotation (cf. Antonio Fomez, From Ruoppolo to Me, Studio Annunciata, Milan, 1982).

To give the reader (for concept of "reader" cf. D. Coste, "Three concepts of the reader and their contribution to a theory of literary texts," Orbis literatum 34, 1880; W. Iser, *Der Akt des Lesens*, München, 1972; *Der implizite Leser*, München, 1976; U. Eco, *Lector in fabula*, Milano, 1979; G. Prince, "Introduction à l'étude du narrataire," *Poétique* 14, 1973; M. Nojgaard, "Le lecteur et la critique," *Degrés* 21, 1980) some creative intuitions (cf. B. Croce, *Estetica come scienza dell'espressione e linguistica generale*, Bari, 1902; H. Bergson, *Oeuvres*, Edition du Centenaire, Paris, 1963; E. Husserl, *Ideen zu einer Phänomenologie und phänomenologischen Philosophie*, Den Haag, 1950) about the painting (for the concept of "painting" cf. Cennino Cennini, *Trattato della pittura*; Bellori, *Vite d'artisti*; Vasari, *Le vite*; P. Barocchi (ed.), *Trattati d'arte del Cinquecento*, Bari, 1960; Lomazzo, *Trattato dell'arte della pittura*; Alberti, *Della pittura*; Armenini, *De' veri precetti della pittura*; Baldinucci, *Vocabolario toscano dell'arte del disegno*; S. van Hoogstraaten, *Inleyding tot de Hooge Schoole der Schilderkonst*, 1678, VIII, 1, pp. 279 et seq.; L. Dolce, *Dialogo della pittura*; Zuccari, *Idea de' pittori*) of Antonio Fomez (cf., for a general bibliography, G. Pedicini, *Fomez*, Milan, 1980, and in particular pp. 60–90), I should essay an analysis (cf. H. Putnam, "The analytic and the synthetic," in *Mind, language, and reality* 2, London and Cambridge, 1975; M. White (ed.), *The Age of Analysis*, New York, 1955) in a form (cf. W. Köhler, *Gestalt Psychology*, New York, 1947; P. Guillaume, *La psychologie de la forme*, Paris, 1937) that is absolutely innocent and unbiased (cf. J. Piaget, *La représentation du monde chez l'enfant*, Paris, 1955; G. Kanizsa, *Grammatica del vedere*, Bologna, 1981). But this is a thing (for the thing in itself, cf. I. Kant, *Kritik der reinen Vernunft*, 1781–1787) that is very difficult in this world (cf. Aristotle, *Metaphysics*) of the post-modern (cf. cf. ((cf. (((cf. cf.)))))). Hence I will do nothing (cf. Sartre, *L'être et le néant*, Paris, 1943). The rest is silence (Wittgenstein, *Tractatus*, 7). Sorry, maybe some other (cf. Lacan, *Ecrits*, Paris, 1966) time (cf. J. B. Priestley, *Time and the Conways*, London, 1937; J. Hilton, *Lost Horizons*, London, 1933).

How to Set the Record Straight

Letter to the Editor

Dear Sir:

With reference to the article by Vera O'Verity entitled "Ides Murder Suspect Denies All" in yesterday's issue, I would like to set the record straight about several matters.

First of all, it is not true that I was present at the assassination of Julius Caesar. As you can see for yourself from the enclosed birth certificate, I was born in Molfetta on March 15, 1944, many centuries, therefore, after the unfortunate event, which, for that matter, I have always deplored. Hence your Ms. O'Verity must have misunderstood when I told her that, with a few friends, I always celebrate the anniversary of March 15—my birthday.

Further, it is similarly incorrect to quote me as

saying later to a certain Brutus, "We will meet at Philippi," or words to that effect. I have never had any contacts with this Mr. Brutus, whose name I heard yesterday for the first time. In the course of our brief telephone interview, I did indeed tell Ms. O'Verity that I would soon be meeting the traffic commissioner, Mr. Filippi, but I mentioned this in the course of discussing the city's traffic problems. In this context, I never said I was hiring some killers to eliminate "that traitor Caesar"; what I said was, "We'd have to be a bunch of maniacs not to take a stab at banning traffic around Caesar Plaza. . . ."

Respectfully yours,
Frank Tawk

Vera O'Verity replies:

Nothing in Mr. Tawk's letter alters the fact that Julius Caesar was assassinated on the Ides of March in '44. I can readily believe that Mr. Tawk and his friends always celebrate the anniversary of March 15, '44. In fact, it was information revealing this suspect behavior that inspired my article. Mr. Tawk may well have personal reasons to propose festive toasts on that date, but even he must agree that the coincidence is, at the very least, curious. He will further recall that, in the course of our long, in-depth telephone interview, he said the words, "I always believe in rendering unto Caesar that which is Caesar's." A source very close to Mr. Tawk—whose good reliability I have no reason to question—has assured me that what was rendered to Caesar was twenty-three stab wounds.

I notice that throughout his letter Mr. Tawk takes care to avoid saying who finally was responsible for those wounds. As for the pathetic "rectification" concerning Philippi, I have before my eyes the notebook in which I wrote, beyond any question, that Mr. Tawk did not say: "I'll be seeing Mr. Filippi." What he said was: "I will see thee at Philippi."

I can similarly confirm the threats uttered against Julius Caesar. The jottings in my notebook, which I am consulting as I write, say clearly: "A bunch of maniacs ... stab at ... Caesar. . . ." Splitting hairs and mincing words cannot absolve Mr. Tawk of his grave responsibilities; nor will his pathetic attempts succeed in gagging our free press.

1988

How to Watch Out for Widows

It may be, dear writers, both male and female, that posterity is of no importance to you; but I don't believe it. Anyone, even the sixteen-year-old who pens a poem about the rustling forest, or the woman who keeps a lifelong diary, merely recording "dentist's appointment this morning," hopes that posterity will cherish those words. For, even if some authors actually desired oblivion, today's publishers are irrepressible in the rediscovery of "forgotten minor writers," even when these never actually wrote a single line.

Posterity, as we know, is voracious and easily pleased. In order to have something to write about, any writing by others will do. Therefore, O writers, you must beware of the use that posterity may make of your work. Naturally, the ideal course would be to leave lying around only the things that, in your lifetime, you had decided to publish, shredding daily any other documentation, including third galleys. But, as we also know, keeping notes as you work is necessary, and death can arrive unexpectedly.

When it does, the first risk is that unpublished material will be published, and will reveal that you were a perfect idiot. And if everyone reads the notes written in the notebook the day before you died, this risk is very strong indeed (particularly because the notes are, inevitably, out of context).

In the absence of notes and notebooks, the second risk is that, immediately post mortem, there will be an epidemic of conferences about your work. Every writer wants to be remembered in essays, doctoral dissertations, critical editions; but these things take time and cash. The immediate conference achieves two results. First, it inspires hordes of friends, admirers, young people in search of fame, to scribble hasty reinterpretations—but, as we know, in such cases they dish up only the familiar gruel, confirming a stereotype. And then, in no time, readers fall out of love with writers so blatantly obvious.

The third risk is that private letters will be published. Writers rarely write private letters that differ from those of ordinary mortals, unless the letters are a pretense, as in the case of Foscolo. They can write "Send me some Preparation H" or "I love you like crazy and I thank God that you exist"—which is only normal and natural, and it is pathetic that posterity should seek out these documents simply to conclude that the writer was a human being. What did you think he or she was? A flamingo?

How can such misfortunes be avoided? With notes and notebooks, I would suggest leaving them in an unlikely place, while abandoning in a desk drawer a kind of buried-treasure map indicating the existence of these documents but with undecipherable directions for finding them. This ensures both that the manuscripts will remain hidden and that many dissertations will be written on the sphinx-like impenetrability of those maps.

As for conferences: it might be a good idea to leave precise testamentary instructions, asking, in the name of Humankind, that for every conference held within ten years of your death, the organizers donate twenty million dollars to UNICEF. It will be hard to raise the sum, and few will be so brazen as to go against the express wishes of the deceased.

The love-letter problem is more complex. For those yet to be written it is a good idea to use the computer, thus thwarting graphologists; sign them with affectionate nicknames ("Your puppy dog, Furrikins"), changing names for each lover, so attribution will prove problematical. It is also advisable to include phrases that, however impassioned, are embarrassing for the addressee ("I love everything about you, even your flatulence"), who will thus be dissuaded from publishing.

Letters already written, especially during adolescence, are beyond revision, however. For these, the best course is to track down the recipient and write a note recalling in tranquillity those bygone days, and promising that even after your death you will revisit the scene, still in the thrall of those memories. This doesn't always work, but a ghost is, after all, a ghost; and the recipient will not sleep well after that.

You could also keep a fake diary, including occasional suggestions that friends and lovers had a tendency to invent and to falsify. "What a delightful liar dear Adelaide is," or "Today Reginald showed me a fake letter from Pessoa: a really admirable job."

1990

How to Organize a Public Library

1. The various catalogues must be housed as far apart as possible from one another. All care must be taken to separate the catalogue of books from that of periodicals, and these two from the catalogue by subject; similarly, the recent acquisitions must be kept well away from older collections. If possible, the spelling in the two catalogues (recent acquisitions and older collections) must be different. In the recent acquisitions, for example, *pajama* should be spelled with an *a*, in the older, *pyjama* with a *y*. *Chaĭkovskiĭ* in recent acquisitions will follow the Library of Congress system; in the older catalogue the name will be spelled in the old-fashioned way, with *Tch*.

2. The subjects must be determined by the librarian. On their copyright pages the books must bear no indication of the subjects under which they are to be listed.

3. Call numbers should be impossible to decipher and, if possible, very complex, so that anyone filling out a call slip will never have room to include the last line of numbers and will assume they are irrelevant. Then the desk attendant will hand the slip back to him with the admonition to fill it out properly.

4. The time between request and delivery must be as long as possible.

5. Only one book should be released at a time.

6. The books distributed by the attendant after the request form has been properly submitted cannot be taken into the reference room, so the scholars must divide their working life into two fundamental aspects: reading, on the one hand, and reference consultation on the other. The library must discourage, as conducive to strabismus, any crossover tendencies or attempts at the simultaneous reading of several books.

7. Insofar as possible, no photocopier should be available; if such a machine does exist, access to it must be made very time-consuming and toilsome, fees should be higher than those in any neighborhood copy shop, and the maximum number of copied pages permitted should not exceed two or three.

8. The librarian must consider the reader an enemy, a waster of time (otherwise he or she would be at work), and a potential thief.

9. The reference librarian's office must be impregnable.

10. Loans must be discouraged.

11. Interlibrary loans must be impossible or, at best, must require months. The idea course, in any event, is to ensure the impossibility of discovering the contents of other libraries.

12. Given this policy, theft must be very easy.

13. Opening hours must coincide precisely with local office hours, determined by foresighted discussions with trade union officials and the Chamber of Commerce; total closing on Saturday, Sunday, evenings and mealtimes goes without saying. The library's worst enemy is the employed student; its best friend is Thomas Jefferson, someone who has a large personal library and therefore no need to visit the public library (to which he may nevertheless bequeath his books at his death).

14. It must be impossible to find any refreshment inside the library, under any circumstances; and it must also be impossible to leave the library to seek sustenance elsewhere without first returning all books in use, so that after having a cup of coffee, the student must fill out requests for them again.

15. It must be impossible on a given day to find the book one had been using the day before.

16. It must be impossible to learn who has a book that is currently out on loan.

17. If possible, no rest rooms.

18. Ideally, the reader should be unable to enter the library. If he does actually enter, exploiting with tedious insistence a right, granted on the basis of the principles of 1789, that has nevertheless not been assimilated by the collective sensibility, he must never ever—with the exception of rapid visits to the reference shelves—be allowed access to the sanctum of the stacks.

CONFIDENTIAL NOTE: All staff must be affected by physical defects, as it is the duty of a public institution to offer job opportunities to handicapped citizens (the Fire Department is considering an extension of this rule to their ranks). In particular, the ideal librarian should limp, in order to lengthen the time devoted to receiving the call slip, descending into the basement, and returning. For personnel expected to use ladders to reach the shelves more than eight meters above the ground, it is required that missing arms be replaced by prosthetic hooks, for security reasons. Personnel lacking both upper limbs will deliver the requested volume by gripping it in their teeth (library regulations tend to prevent the delivery of volumes in a format larger than octavo).

1981

How to Speak of Animals

Central Park. The zoo. Some kids are playing near the polar bear tank. One dares the others to dive into the tank and swim alongside the bears; to force them to dive in, the challenger hides the others' clothes; the boys enter the water, splashing past a big male bear, peaceful and drowsy; they tease him, he becomes annoyed, extends a paw, and eats, or rather chomps on, two kids, leaving some bits lying around. The police come quickly, even the mayor arrives, there is some argument about whether or not the bear has to be killed, all admit it's not his fault; some sensational articles appear in the press. It so happens that the boys have Hispanic names: Puerto Ricans, perhaps black, perhaps newcomers to the city, in any event accustomed to feats of daring, like all slum kids who hang out in packs.

Various interpretations ensue, all fairly severe. The

cynical reaction is fairly widespread, at least in conversation: natural selection, if they were stupid enough to mess with a bear, they got what they deserved; even when I was five, I had enough sense not to jump into a bear tank. Social interpretation: areas of poverty, insufficient education, alas, the subproletariat has a tendency to act on impulse, without thinking. But, I ask you, what's all this talk about insufficient education? Even the poorest child watches TV, or has read a schoolbook in which bears devour humans and hunters therefore kill bears.

At this point I began to wonder if the boys didn't venture into the pool precisely because they do watch TV and go to school. These children were probably victims of our guilty conscience, as reflected in the schools and the mass media.

Human beings have always been merciless with animals, but when humans became aware of their own cruelty, they began, if not to love all animals (because, with only sporadic hesitation, they continue eating them), at least to speak well of them. As the media, the schools, public institutions in general, have to explain away so many acts performed against humans by humans, it seems finally a good idea, psychologically and ethically, to insist on the goodness of animals. We allow children of the Third World to die, but we urge children of the First to respect not only butterflies and bunny rabbits but also whales, crocodiles, snakes.

Mind you, this educational approach is per se correct. What is excessive is the persuasive technique chosen: to render animals worthy of rescue they are humanized, toyified. No one says they are entitled to survive *even if*, as a rule, they are savage and carnivorous. No, they are made respectable by becoming cuddly, comic, good-natured, benevolent, wise, and prudent.

No one is more thoughtless than a lemming, more deceitful than a cat, more slobbering than a dog in August, more smelly than a piglet, more hysterical than a horse, more idiotic than a moth, more slimy than a snail, more poisonous than a viper, less imaginative than an ant, and less musically creative than a nightingale. Simply put, we must love—or, if that is downright impossible, at least respect—these and other animals for what they are. The tales of earlier times overdid the wicked wolf, the tales of today exaggerate the good wolves. We must save the whales, not because they are good, but because they are a part of nature's inventory and they contribute to the ecological equilibrium. Instead, our children are raised with whales that talk, wolves that join the Third Order of St. Francis, and, above all, an endless array of teddy bears.

Advertising, cartoons, illustrated books are full of bears with hearts of gold, law-abiding, cozy, and protective—although in fact it's insulting for a bear to be told he has a right to live because he's only a dumb but inoffensive brute. So I suspect that the poor children in Central Park died not through lack of education but through too much of it. They are the victims of our unhappy conscience.

To make them forget how bad human beings are, they were taught too insistently that bears are good. Instead of being told honestly what humans are and what bears are.

1987

How
to Play
Indians

Since the future of Native American culture at present seems dire, the sole possibility for the young brave bent on improving his social position is to appear in a Western movie. To assist him in this endeavor, we offer some essential guidelines, tips on correct behavior in both war and peace situations, to help him qualify as "movie Indian," thus providing as well a solution to the problem of underemployment among members of this beleaguered minority.

Before Attacking

1. Never attack immediately: make yourself visible at a distance a few days ahead of time, producing easily-observed smoke signals, thus giving the stagecoach or the fort ample time to send word to the Seventh Cavalry.

2. If possible, appear prominently in small groups on the surrounding hills. Set up sentinels on totally isolated peaks.

3. Leave clear traces of your progress: hoofprints, smoldering campfires, feathers, and amulets allowing identification of tribe.

Attacking the Stagecoach

4. In any attack on a stagecoach, always follow the vehicle at a short distance or, better still, ride alongside it, to facilitate your being shot.

5. Restrain your mustangs, notoriously faster than coach horses, so you won't outstrip the vehicle.

6. Try to stop the coach single-handed, flinging yourself on the harness, so you can be whipped by the driver and then run over by the vehicle.

7. Never block the coach's advance in a large body. The driver would stop at once.

Attacking an Isolated Farm or a Circle of Covered Wagons

8. Never attack at night when the settlers might not be expecting you. Respect the tradition that Indians attack only in daytime.

9. Insist on making your presence known by giving the coyote cry, thus revealing your position.

10. If a white man gives the coyote cry, raise your head immediately to offer him an easy target.

11. Attack by circling the wagons, but never narrow your circle, so that you and your companions can be picked off one by one.

12. Never employ all your men in a circle, but progressively replace those that fall.

13. As you lack stirrups, manage somehow to entangle your feet in the reins, so that, when you are shot, you are dragged after your mount.

14. Use rifles, bought illegally, whose operation is unfamiliar to you. Take a considerable amount of time loading them.

15. Don't stop circling the wagons when the good guys arrive. Wait for the cavalry without riding out to confront it, then scatter at the first impact in total disorder to allow individual pursuit.

16. In preparing to attack an isolated farm, send only one man to spy on it at night. Approaching a lighted window, he must observe at length a white woman inside, until she has become aware of the Indian face pressed against the pane. Await the woman's cry and the exit of the men before attempting to escape.

Attacking the Fort

17. First of all, turn the horses loose at night. Do not steal them. Encourage them to disperse over the prairie.

18. In using a ladder during the assault, climb up it one man at a time. First allow your weapon to appear, then your head, slowly, and emerge only after the white woman has indicated your presence to a marksman. Never fall forward, inside the fort, but always backward, toward the exterior.

19. In shooting from a distance, assume a clearly visible position on the top of a peak, so that you can fall forward, to be shattered on the rocks below.

20. In the event of a face-to-face confrontation, wait before taking aim.

21. In the same situation, never use a pistol, which would resolve the confrontation at once. Only naked steel.

22. In the case of a sortie on the part of the whites, never steal the weapons of the slain enemy, only his watch. Wait in wonderment, listening to its tick, until another enemy arrives.

23. On capturing an enemy, do not kill him immediately. Tie him to a stake or confine him to a tent, awaiting the new moon, by which time others will come to free him.

24. In any event, you can be certain that the enemy bugler will be killed the moment the signal of the Seventh Cavalry is heard from afar. At this point the bugler inside the fort always stands up and returns the signal from the highest turret of the fort.

Further Instructions

25. In the event that the Indian village is attacked, rush from the tents in total confusion. Run around every which way, trying to collect weapons previously left in places of difficult access.

26. Check the quality of the firewater being sold by the peddlers: the sulfuric acid-to-whisky ratio must be three to one.

27. In the event of a train's passing, make sure there is an Indian hunter on board and ride alongside the train brandishing rifles and emitting cries of greeting.

28. In leaping from a roof to seize a white man from behind, always hold your knife in such a way that he

is not immediately wounded but is allowed to engage in hand-to-hand struggle. Wait until the white man turns around.

1975

How to Recognize a Porn Movie

I don't know if you've ever happened to see a porno-graphic movie. I don't mean movies with some erotic content, a movie like *Last Tango in Paris*, for example, though even that, I realize, for many people might be offensive. No, what I mean is genuine pornoflicks, whose true and sole aim is to stimulate the spectator's desire, from beginning to end, and in such a way that, while this desire is stimulated by scenes of various and varied copulations, the rest of the story counts for less than nothing.

Magistrates are often required to decide whether a film is purely pornographic or whether it has artistic value. I am not one of those who insist that artistic value excuses everything; sometimes true works of art have been more dangerous, to faith, to behavior, to current opinion, than works of lesser value. But I believe that consenting adults have the right to consume pornographic material, at least for want of anything better. I recognize, however, that on occasion a court must decide whether a film has been produced for the purpose of expressing certain concepts or aesthetic ideals (even through scenes that offend the accepted moral view), or whether it was made for the sole purpose of arousing the spectator's instincts.

Well, there is a criterion for deciding whether a film is pornographic or not, and it is based on the calculation of wasted time. A great, universal film masterpiece, *Stagecoach*, takes place solely and entirely (except for the beginning, a few brief intervals, and the finale) on a stagecoach. But without this journey the film would have no meaning. Antonioni's *L'avventura* is made up solely of wasted time: people come and go, talk, get lost and are found, without anything happening. This wasted time may or may not be enjoyable, but it is exactly what the film is about.

A pornographic movie, in contrast, to justify the price of the ticket or the purchase of the cassette, tells us that certain people couple sexually, men with women, men with men, women with women, women with dogs or stallions (I might point out that there are no pornographic films in which men couple with mares and bitches: why not?). And this would still be all right: but it is full of wasted time.

If Gilbert, in order to rape Gilbertina, has to go from Lincoln Center to Sheridan Square, the film shows you Gilbert, in his car, throughout the whole journey, stoplight by stoplight.

Pornographic movies are full of people who climb into cars and drive for miles and miles, couples who waste incredible amounts of time signing in at hotel desks, gentlemen who spend many minutes in eleva-

206

tors before reaching their rooms, girls who sip various drinks and who fiddle interminably with laces and blouses before confessing to each other that they prefer Sappho to Don Juan. To put it simply, crudely, in porn movies, before you can see a healthy screw you have to put up with a documentary that could be sponsored by the Traffic Bureau.

There are obvious reasons. A movie in which Gilbert did nothing but rape Gilbertina, front, back, and sideways, would be intolerable. Physically, for the actors, and economically, for the producer. And it would also be, psychologically, intolerable for the spectator: for the transgression to work, it must be played out against a background of normality. To depict normality is one of the most difficult things for any artist— whereas portraying deviation, crime, rape, torture, is very easy.

Therefore the pornographic movie must present normality—essential if the transgression is to have interest—in the way that every spectator conceives it. Therefore, if Gilbert has to take the bus and go from A to B, we will see Gilbert taking the bus and then the bus proceeding from A to B.

This often irritates the spectators, because they think they would like the unspeakable scenes to be continuous. But this is an illusion on their part. They couldn't bear a full hour and a half of unspeakable scenes. So the passages of wasted time are essential.

I repeat. Go into a movie theater. If, to go from A to B, the characters take longer than you would like, then the film you are seeing is pornographic.

1989

How
to Avoid
Contagious
Diseases

Many years ago a TV actor, who made no secret of his homosexuality, said to a youth whom he was frankly trying to seduce, "You go with women? Don't you know that can cause cancer?" The remark is still quoted around the Milan television studios, but now the time for such joking has passed. I read recently that according to the revelations of Professor Matré, heterosexual contact *is* carcinogenic. High time somebody came out and said it. I would go even farther: heterosexual contact causes death, period. Even a fool knows that it ends in procreation, and the more people are born, the more people die.

With scant regard for democratic principles, the AIDS psychosis threatened to constrict the activity only of homosexuals. Now we will limit heterosexual activity as well, and all of us will once again be on the same footing. But (while I would not want to foster excessive alarmism) I would still like to point out some other high-risk categories.

Drama Critics, Intellectuals, Aspiring Politicians

Do not attend Off-Off-Broadway theaters in New York. It is a known fact that, for phonetic reasons, English-speaking actors spit a great deal. You have only to see them in profile, against the light, to notice this; and experimental theaters seat the spectators directly in the line of the actor's spray. If you are an elected official, have no dealings with mafiosi, or you will have to kiss the godfather's hand. Connections with the camorra are also not advised, in view of the blood rituals. Anyone embarking on a political career through Catholic Action membership must somehow avoid Holy Communion, as germs can be transmitted from mouth to mouth via the fingertips of the celebrant, and the risks of auricular confession are self-evident.

Ordinary Citizens

Swimming in an oil-polluted sea increases the risk of contagion, because the oil droplets transport particles of saliva from other swimmers, who have previously swallowed the polluted liquid and spat it out. Anyone who smokes more than eighty Gauloises a day touches—with fingers that have touched other things—the upper part of all those cigarettes, and the germs enter the respiratory channels. Avoid being fired from your job, because you then spend the day chewing your fingernails. Take care not to be kidnapped by Sardinian shepherds or by terrorists: the kidnappers as a rule use the same hood for many kidnapped victims. Never travel by train between Florence and Bologna, as terrorist explosions in the confined area of the tunnels spread organic detritus very quickly, and in such moments of confusion it is difficult to protect oneself. Avoid areas subject to bombardment by nuclear warheads: faced with the sight of a mushroom cloud, the spectator has an instinctive tendency to put his (unwashed) hands to his mouth, as he murmurs, "My God!"

Further risk is caused by the dying who kiss crucifixes; those sentenced to death (the blade of the guillotine is seldom properly disinfected before reuse); and orphans in institutions, where the wicked nuns make each little malefactor lick the floor, after tying his leg to his cot.

Ethnic Minorities and Inhabitants of the Third World

Native Americans are severely threatened: passing the calumet from mouth to mouth has caused, as everyone knows, the near-extinction of the Indian nation. Citizens of the Middle East and of Afghanistan are exposed to the licking of camels, hence the high mortality rate in Iran and Iraq. A desaparecido runs great risk when his merciless torturers spit in his face. Cambodians and the inhabitants of Lebanese camps should avoid the (blood) bath, discouraged by nine physicians out of ten (the tenth, more open-minded, is Dr. Mengele).

South African blacks are exposed to infection of various kinds when the white man considers them with contempt, grimaces, and ejects saliva. Political prisoners of every color must take great care to elude the backhand slap of the police, striking their teeth after similarly touching the gums of other persons held for questioning. Members of populations subject to endemic famine must try not to swallow frequently in an attempt to allay the pangs of hunger, as their saliva, which has come into contact with the foul air of their surroundings, can contaminate their intestines.

The authorities and the press, instead of printing scandalous headlines about other problems whose solution could reasonably be postponed to some future date, should devote their energies to a campaign of hygienic instruction of the sort indicated here.

1985

How
to Choose
a Remunerative
Profession

There are certain jobs that are much in demand and that pay very well, but they require careful preparation.

For example, the job of setting up around the city those signs that indicate the way to the superhighways. Their purpose is to clear traffic from the downtown area—and also from the superhighways, as we promptly realize once we have followed them and ended up, exhausted, on the most dangerous dead-end street in the industrial suburbs. But it is not easy to put the signs in exactly the right places. A simpleton might consider placing them at a spot where the driver is confronted with a complicated choice among several streets, and where there is thus a good chance he will get lost if left unassisted. But, on the contrary, the sign must be affixed only where, since the proper route is obvious and the driver would instinctively choose it, he must be sent off in another direction. To do the job really well the applicant should have some notion of urban planning, psychology, and the theory of games.

Another very desirable job is that of writing the instructions included in, or printed on, the packaging of domestic appliances and electronic instruments. Above all, these instructions must prevent installation. The ideal model is not that of the thick manuals supplied with computers; these also achieve this aim, but at great cost to the manufacturer. The proper model is rather the folded slip of paper accompanying pharmaceuticals, products with the extra feature of having names that, while apparently scientific, have actually been devised to make obvious the nature of the product as if to ensure that its purchase embarrasses the purchaser (Prostatan, Menopausin, Crabex). The instructions enclosed in the box, in contrast, succeed with a minimum of words in making incomprehensible the warnings on which our lives depend: "No counterindication, except in cases of unforeseen lethal reaction to product."

For domestic appliances et similia the instructions must expound at length things so self-evident that you are tempted to skip them, thus missing the one truly essential bit of information.

In order to install the PZ40 it is necessary to unwrap the packaging and remove the appliance from the box. The PZ40 can be extracted from its container only after the latter is opened. The container is opened by lifting, in opposite directions, the two flaps of the upper side of the box (see diagram below). Take care, during the process of opening, to keep the container in a vertical position, with the lid facing up, otherwise the PZ40 may fall out during the operation and suffer damage. The lid to be opened is clearly marked with the words THIS SIDE UP. In the event that the lid does not open at the first attempt, the consumer is advised to try a second time. Once the lid is opened, it is advisable to tear off the red strip before removing the inner, aluminum lid; otherwise the container will explode. WARNING: after the PZ40 has been removed, the container can be discarded.

Another job that is not to be dismissed lightly is that of compiling questionnaires, usually during the summer season, for popular weekly magazines. "Between a bottle of Epsom salts and one of twenty-year-old cognac, which would you choose? Would you rather spend your vacation with an eighty-year-old leper or with Demi Moore? Do you prefer being sprinkled with ferocious red ants or sharing a sleeping compartment with Claudia Schiffer? If you have answered '1' to all the above questions, then you are inventive, original, brilliant, but sexually a bit frigid. If all your answers are '2', then you're a rascal."

In the Medicine and Health supplement of a leading daily I came upon a questionnaire about sunbathing, which allowed you to choose among three answers for every question, A, B, and C. The A answers are interesting: "If you expose your skin to the sun, how red does it get? A: Intensely. How often do you suffer from sunburn? A: Every time I go out in the sun. How would you describe your skin forty-eight hours after the erythema? A: Still red. Solution: if you have answered A to most questions, your skin is very sensitive and you are subject to painful sunburn." I am thinking of a questionnaire that would ask: "Have you often fallen out of a window? If yes, have you suffered multiple fractures? After each fall, have you been certified as permanently disabled? If your answers are A, either you're pretty stupid or your aural labyrinth is in bad shape. Don't look out the window when the usual jokester yells up from below urging you to come down and join him."

1991

The Miracle
of San Baudolino

Barbarians

Dante does not treat my native Alessandria with great tenderness in his *De vulgari eloquentia*, where, in recording the dialects of the Italian peninsula, he declares that the "hirsute" sounds emitted by our people are surely not an Italian dialect and implies they are barely acceptable as a language. All right, so we're barbarians. But this, too, is a vocation.

We are not Italians (Latins), nor are we Celts. We are the descendants of Ligurian tribes, tough and hairy, and in 1856 Carlo Avalle, beginning his history of Piedmont, recalled what Virgil said of those pre-Roman Italic peoples in Book IX of the *Aeneid*:

> And what sort of people did you think to find here?
> Those perfumed Atridae or the double-talking
> Ulysses?

You have come upon a people harsh from birth.
Our children, barely-born, are cast into the icy rivers,
whose waves toughen them first,
then through mountain and forests
the youth go day and night . . .

Et cetera. Avalle says further that these barbarians "were thin and undistinguished of person, having soft skin, small eyes, sparse hair, gaze filled with pride, harsh and loud voice: thus, at first sight, they did not give an accurate indication of their exceptional strength . . . ."

One woman, it is said, was "seized by the pangs of birth while she was at work. Giving no sign, she went and hid behind a thorn bush. Having given birth there, she covered the infant with leaves, and returned to her tasks, and so no one noticed. But when the babe began to cry, the mother's secret was revealed. Yet, deaf to the urgings of friends and companions, she did not cease working until the master obliged her to, after giving her her wage. This episode inspired the saying, often repeated by historians, that among the Ligurians the women had the strength of men, and the men, the strength of wild beasts." This was written by Diodorus Siculus.

On the Field of Marengo

The hero of Alessandria is named Gagliaudo. In the year 1168, Alessandria exists and yet it doesn't; that is to say, it doesn't exist under that name. It is a collection of hamlets, perhaps, a fortified settlement or castle. In the area live some peasants and perhaps some of those *mercatanti* (merchants) who, as Carducci was to say later, will appear to the German feudal lords as unacceptable adversaries who "only yesterday girded their paunches with knightly steel." The Italian communes join forces against Barbarossa, forming the Lombard League; and they decide to build a new city at the confluence of the Tanaro and the Bormida, to block the advance of the invader.

The people of those scattered hamlets accept the proposal, probably because they can see a number of advantages. They seem only to be concerned with their private interests, but when Barbarossa arrives, they stand fast, and Barbarossa is stopped. It is 1174, Barbarossa is pressing at the gates, Alessandria is starving, and then (the legend goes) the wily Gagliaudo appears, a peasant who might be a relative of Schwejk. He makes the richest men in the city give him what little wheat they can manage to collect, he gorges his cow Rosina on it, and leads her outside the walls to graze. Naturally, Barbarossa's men capture her, disembowel her, and are stunned to find her so stuffed with grain. And Gagliaudo, an expert in playing dumb, tells Barbarossa that in the city there is so much wheat that they have to use it to feed the livestock. Let's go back for a moment to Carducci: picture his army of romantics who weep at night, the bishop of Spires who dreams of the beautiful towers of his cathedral, the paladin Count of the blond locks who now despairs of ever seeing his Thecla again, all of them mortified at the thought of having "to die at the hand of *mercatanti* ...." Then the German army strikes its tents and goes off.

This is how the legend goes. In reality, the siege was bloodier. It seems that the communal militia of my city performed well on the battlefield, but the city prefers to celebrate as its hero this sly and unbloody peasant, a bit short on military talent, but guided by one radiant certitude: that everyone else was a bit more stupid than he.

Po Valley Epiphanies

I know I am beginning these memoirs in a very Alessandrian spirit, but I would be unable to think up a presentation more—how shall I put it?—monumental. Actually, in describing a "flat" city like Alessandria, I believe the monumental approach is mistaken; I prefer to proceed along more subdued lines. I will tell about some epiphanies. The epiphany (I quote Joyce) is like a "sudden spiritual manifestation . . ." either in "the vulgarity of speech or of gesture or in a memorable phrase of the mind itself." A dialogue, a city clock emerging from the evening fog, a whiff of rotting cabbage, something insignificant that suddenly becomes important: these were the epiphanies Joyce recorded in his foggy Dublin. And Alessandria resembles Dublin more than it does Constantinople.

It was a spring morning in 1943. The decision had been made: we were definitely going to abandon the city. Moreover, the splendid plan was to take refuge at Nizza Monferrato, where we would surely avoid the air raids. (A few months later, however, caught in crossfire between Fascists and partisans, I would learn to jump into ditches to duck the Sten guns' fire.) Now it was early morning, and we were heading for the station, the whole family, in a hired carriage. At the point where Corso Cento Cannoni opens towards the Valfré barracks, the broad space deserted at this early hour, I thought I glimpsed, in the distance, Rossini, my elementary school classmate, and I called to him in a loud voice. It was someone else. My father was irritated. He said that, as usual, I never stopped to think, and one doesn't go around shouting "Verdini" like a lunatic. I corrected him, saying the name was Rossini, and he said that, Verdini or Bianchini, it was all the same. A few months later, when Alessandria was subjected to its first bombing, I learned that Rossini had died beneath the rubble with his mother.

Epiphanies should not be explained, but in the above recollection there are at least three of them. First, I was scolded for having succumbed to excessive enthusiasm. Second, I had thoughtlessly uttered a name. In Alessandria, every year they put on *Gelindo*, a pastoral Christmas story. The story takes place in Bethlehem, but the shepherds speak and debate in Alessandrian dialect. Only the Roman centurions, St. Joseph, and the Magi speak standard Italian (and in so doing seem highly comical). Now Medoro, one of Gelindo's servants, encounters the Magi and imprudently tells them the name of his master. When Gelindo finds out, he flies into a rage and scolds Medoro roundly. You don't tell your own name to just anyone and you don't thoughtlessly call somebody else by name, out in the open, where everyone can hear. An Alessandrian may talk with you for a whole day without once calling you by name, not even when he greets you. You say "Ciao" or, on separating, "Arrivederci," never "Arrivederci, Giuseppe."

The third epiphany is more ambiguous. In my memory I can still see that urban space, too broad, like a jacket handed down from father to son, where that little human form stood out, too distant from our carriage: an ambiguous meeting with a friend I was never to see again. In the flat and excessive spaces of

Alessandria you become lost. When the city is really deserted, early in the morning, at night, or on the Ferragosto holiday (or even any Sunday at around 1:30 P.M.), the way from one place to another, in this tiny city, is always too long, and all of it is in the open, where anyone in ambush behind a corner, or in a passing carriage, might see you, invade your privacy, shout your name, ruin you forever. Alessandria is more vast than the Sahara, with faded Morgan le Fays crossing it in every direction.

This is why the people talk very little, merely exchanging rapid signals; they lose you (and themselves). This conditions relationships, hatreds as much as loves. Alessandria, as an urban entity, has no gathering points (or perhaps just one, Piazzetta della Lega), but it has *dispersion points* almost everywhere. For this reason you never know who's there and who isn't.

I am reminded of a story that isn't Alessandrian, but could be. At the age of twenty Salvatore leaves his native town and emigrates to Australia, where he lives as an exile for forty years. Then, at sixty, having saved his money, he comes home. And as the train approaches the station, Salvatore daydreams: Will he find his old friends, the comrades of the past, in the café of his youth? Will they recognize him? Will they make a fuss over him, ask him with eager curiosity to tell them his adventures among the kangaroos and the aboriginals? And that girl who once . . .? And the shopkeeper on the corner . . .? And so on.

The train pulls into the deserted station, Salvatore steps onto the platform under the blazing noonday sun. In the distance there is a hunched little man, a railway worker. Salvatore takes a better look; he recognizes that man, despite the bent shoulders, the face lined with forty years of wrinkles: why, of course, it's Giovanni, his friend, his schoolmate! He waves to him, anxiously approaches, and with trembling hand points to his own face, as if to say: it's me. Giovanni looks at him, shows no sign of recognition, then thrusts out his chin in a greeting: "Hey there, Salvatore, where are you off to?"

In the great Alessandrian desert adolescence can be fevered. 1942, I am on my bike, between two and five on a July afternoon. I am looking for something: from the Citadel to the Track, then from the Track to the Gardens, and from the Gardens towards the station. I cut across Piazza Garibaldi, circumnavigate the Penitentiary, and head off again towards the Tanaro, but this time going through the city center. Nobody to be seen. I have a firm destination, the station magazine stand where I have seen a cheap paperback edition, no longer new, of a story, translated from the French, that looks fascinating. It costs one lira, and I have exactly one lira in my pocket. Shall I buy it, or not? The other shops are closed, or seem to be. My friends are on vacation. Alessandria is only space, sun, a track for my bike with its pocked tires; the little book at the station is the only hope of narrative, and hence of reality. (Many years later I would have a kind of *intermittence du coeur*, a short circuit between memory and present image, landing in a wobbling plane in the center of Brazil, at São Jesus da Lapa. The plane couldn't land because two sleepy dogs were stretched out in the middle of the cement runway, and they wouldn't move. What is the connection? None. This is how epiphanies work.)

But that day, that day of long foreplay between me

and the little book, the duel between my desire and the sultry resistance of the Alessandrian space (and who knows if the book wasn't only the screen, the mask of other desires that were already unnerving a body and an imagination that were neither flesh nor fowl?), that long amorous pedaling in the summer void, that circling flight, remain for all their awfulness a memory heartrending in its sweetness and, I would say, in its ethnic pride. This is how we are, like the city. To end the story, if you want me to, I finally made up my mind and bought the little book. As I recall, it was an imitation of the *Atlantide* of Pierre Benoît, but with an extra dash of Verne. As the sun set, I was shut up in the house, but I had already left Alessandria, I was navigating on the bed of silent seas, I was witnessing other sunsets and other horizons. My father, coming home, remarked that I read too much and said to my mother that I should spend more time outdoors. But, on the contrary, I was curing myself of the excess of space.

Never Exaggerate

I had a shock when, a bit older, I entered the university in Turin. The Turinese are French, or in any case Celts, not Ligurian barbarians like us. My new companions arrived in the halls of Palazzo Campana in the morning, wearing a proper shirt and a proper tie, they smiled at me and approached with hand extended: "Ciao, how are you?" Nothing like this had ever happened to me before. In Alessandria, when I ran into companions busy holding up a wall, they would look at me through half-closed eyelids and say, with shy cordiality, "Hey there, stupid!" Ninety kilometers away, and here was a different civilization. I am still so steeped in it that I persist in considering it superior. In our parts, you don't lie.

When somebody shot at Togliatti there was great unrest: the Alessandrians do get excited, on occasion. They filled Piazza della Libertà, the former Piazza Rattazzi. But then the radio was heard from the loudspeakers, spreading the news of Gino Bartali's victory in the Tour de France. This superb mass-media operation, we learned afterwards, worked throughout Italy. In Alessandria it didn't work quite well enough: we are too smart, you can't make us forget about Togliatti by broadcasting news of a bicycle race. But then, suddenly, an airplane appeared over city hall. This may have been the first time a plane flew over Alessandria with an advertising banner (I don't remember what it was advertising); this was no diabolical stratagem: it was chance. The Alessandrian distrusts diabolical stratagems, but he is very indulgent towards chance. The crowd watched the plane: here's something a bit unusual, why, what will they think up next, they come up with a new one every minute. With detachment everyone expressed his opinion, his personal, profound conviction that, in any case, the matter would have no influence on the general curve of entropy or on the heat death of the universe—these aren't their exact words, but this idea is always implicit in every word spoken in our Alessandrian dialect. Then everybody went home, because the day had no more surprises in store. Togliatti would have to fend for himself.

I imagine that these stories, told to others (I mean, to non-Alessandrians), can be appalling. I find them sublime. I find them the equal of other sublime epiphanies offered us by the history of a city that manages to get itself built with the help of the pope and the Lombard League, resists Barbarossa out of pigheadedness, but then doesn't take part in the Battle of Legnano. A city of which one legend tells how a queen called Pedoca comes from Germany to besiege; on her arrival, she plants some vineyards, saying she won't leave before she has drunk the wine made from their grapes. The siege lasts for seven years, but a sequel to the legend says that Pedoca, defeated by the Alessandrians, pours onto the barren earth the wine from her cask in a furious ritual of rage and destruction, as if offering up a great and barbaric blood sacrifice. Pedoca, imaginative and poetic queen, punishes herself, renouncing her own pleasure in order to get drunk on massacre, even if it is only symbolic.... The Alessandrians look on, take note, and derive, as their only conclusion, a way of indicating a person's stupidity, the expression "Furb c'm' Pedoca" (clever like Pedoca).

Alessandria, where St. Francis passes by and converts a wolf, as he did in Gubbio; but while Gubbio makes a big fuss over the event, Alessandria forgets. What is a saint supposed to do, if not convert wolves? And besides, how could they, the Alessandrians, understand this Umbrian visitor, a bit histrionic, and a bit hysterical, who talks to birds instead of going out and working?

Interested in their trade, the Alessandrians get into quarrels and wage wars. In 1282 they steal the chains from a bridge in Pavia and display them in the Duomo as a trophy; but after a while, the sacristan uses them to fix the fireplace in his kitchen and nobody notices. They sack Casale, steal the angel from the spire of the cathedral, but, somehow or other, they end up losing it.

If you leaf through the opening pages of the *Guide to the Italy of Legend and Fantasy*, where a series of charts illustrates the distribution of fantastic beings in the provinces of northern Italy, you will see that the province of Alessandria stands out thanks to its virginity. It has no witches, devils, fairies, sprites, mages, monsters, ghosts, caves, labyrinths, or buried treasure, saving its reputation thanks only to one "bizarre construction." You have to admit that's pretty slim pickings.

Distrust of mystery. Distrust of the noumenon. A city wihout ideals and without passions. In a period when nepotism is a virtue, Pius V, the Alessandrian-born pope, drives his relations out of Rome and tells them to look out for themselves. Inhabited for centuries by a rich Jewish community, Alessandria can't even work up enough energy to become anti-Semitic, and ignores the injunction of the Inquisition. The Alessandrians have never worked up any enthusiasm for a heroic cause, not even one preaching the necessity of exterminating those who are different. Alessandria has never felt the need to impose a Verbum by force of arms; it has given us no linguistic models for radio announcers, it has created no miracles of art that could inspire subscriptions to save them, it has never had anything to teach other nations, it has nothing for its sons to be proud of, nothing it has ever bothered to be proud of itself.

But how proud people can feel, discovering themselves to be children of a city without bombast and without myths, without missions and without truths.

226

Understanding Fog

Alessandria is made up of great spaces. It is empty. And sleepy. But all of a sudden, on certain evenings in autumn or winter, when the city is submerged in fog, the voids vanish, and from the milky grayness, in the beams of headlights, corners, edges, unexpected facades, dark perspectives emerge from nothingness, in a new play of nuanced forms, and Alessandria becomes "beautiful." A city made to be seen in half-light, as you grope along, sticking to the walls. You must look for its identity not in sunshine but in haze. In the fog you walk slowly, you have to know the way if you don't want to get lost; but you always, somehow, arrive somewhere.

Fog is good and loyally rewards those who know it and love it. Walking in fog is better than walking in snow, trampling it down with hobnailed boots, because the fog comforts you not only from below but also from above, you don't soil it, you don't destroy it, it enfolds you affectionately and resumes its form after you have passed. It fills your lungs like a good tobacco; it has a strong and healthy aroma; it strokes your cheeks and slips between your lapels and your chin, tickling your neck, it allows you to glimpse from the distance ghosts that dissolve as you move closer, or it lets you suddenly discern in front of you forms, perhaps real, that dodge you and disappear into the emptiness. (Unfortunately, what you really need is a permanent war, with a blackout; it is only in such times that the fog is at its best, but you can't always have everything.) In the fog you are sheltered against the outside world, face to face with your inner self. *Nebulat ergo cogito.*

Luckily, when there is no fog on the Alessandrian plain, especially in the early morning, *scarnebbia*, as we say; it "unfogs." A kind of nebulous dew, instead of illuminating the fields, rises to confuse sky and earth, lightly moistening your face. Now—in contrast to the foggy days—visibility is excessive, but the landscape remains sufficiently monochrome; everything is washed in delicate hues of gray and nothing offends the eye. You have to go outside the city, along the secondary roads or, better, along the paths flanking a straight canal, on a bicycle, without a scarf, a newspaper stuffed under your jacket to protect your chest. On the fields of Marengo, open to the moon and where, dark between the Bormida and the Tanaro, a forest stirs and lows, two battles were won long ago (1174 and 1800), the climate is invigorating.

San Baudolino

The patron saint of Alessandria is Baudolino ("O San Baudolino—from heaven protect—our diocese and its faithful elect"). This is his story, as told by Paulus Diaconus:

In Liutprand's times, in a place that was called Foro, near the Tanaro, there shone a man of wondrous sanctity, who with the help of Christ's grace worked many miracles, and he often predicted the future and spoke of distant things as if they were present. Once, when the king had come to hunt in the forest of Orba, it so happened that one of his men, having taken aim at a stag, with his arrow wounded the nephew of the same king, the little son of his sister, by the name of Anphuso. Seeing this, Liutprand, who greatly loved the boy, began to

228

weep over his misfortune and immediately sent one of his knights to the man of God, Baudolino, begging him to implore Christ to spare the life of the unhappy boy.

Here I will interrupt the quotation for a moment, to allow the reader to make his own predictions. What would a normal saint—not an Alessandrian, in other words—have done in this situation? Now we will resume the story, again giving Paulus the floor:

As the knight set off, the boy died. Whereupon the prophet, seeing the man arrive, spoke to him thus: "I know the reason why you have come, but what you ask is impossible, because the boy is already dead." On hearing these words, the king, distresssed though he was at not having his prayer answered, still openly recognized that Baudolino, the man of the Lord, was gifted with the spirit of prophecy.

I would say that Liutprand behaves well and understands the lesson of a great saint. Which is that, in real life, you can't perform too many miracles. And the wise man is he who bears necessity in mind. Baudolino performs another miracle: convincing a credulous Langobard that miracles are rare merchandise.

1965–90